ABOUT WOOCOMMERCE EXP

My name is Patrick Rauland and I'm obsessed with WooCommerce. I used the product as a customer, joined the WooCommerce team and did a variety of roles, and now I teach it to others.

Throughout this book, we'll refer to "we" and "us." This book was a team effort. Thanks to Steve Burge who helped with the writing and Topher DeRosia who worked on the original training material. And, thanks to you for reading! You are part of our WooCommerce team!

We've worked with WooCommerce users in many cities and countries. We've met lots of different types of WooCommerce users:

- WooCommerce users come from many different backgrounds. They are accountants, florists, photographers, secretaries, factory workers, stay-at-home parents, and people from all walks of life.

- WooCommerce users don't need to know anything about websites. Some WooCommerce learners are professional web designers, but many others have never built a site before and don't know any website code or jargon.

- WooCommerce users don't need any experience. We've trained people who went to work the previous week and found their boss saying, "Surprise! You're running our WooCommerce site!" They often still wore their look of surprise.

- WooCommerce users are of all ages. We've taught 15-year old students skipping class all the way up to retirees who are over 80.

If any of those descriptions sound like you, you've picked up the right book. WooCommerce lets you build your own online store.

Using plain English and straightforward instructions, this book will help teach you how to build great websites using WooCommerce.

THIS BOOK IS ACTIVE

You don't learn to ride a bicycle by reading a book: You learn by actually riding.

You don't learn to drive a car by reading a book: You learn by actually driving.

A book can help and give some advice, but without actually riding a bike or driving a car, you'll never really learn. The same is true with WooCommerce.

So, throughout almost every chapter of this book, you're going to be asked to work with WooCommerce.

The WooCommerce logo and all of the branding uses the color purple. Since we're making a book about WooCommerce, we thought we'd make a store called **Purpleville** that sells everything purple. We're going to sell some simple products and some complex products, all of which are designed to show off different features within WooCommerce.

THIS BOOK WILL LEAVE SOME THINGS OUT

Big books are no fun. They're expensive to buy, heavy to carry, and often written in long, complicated sentences, paragraphs, and chapters that go on and on while the text grows and the words grow longer and more obscure as the author tries to show their verbosity and vocabulary, examining the thesaurus for words that describe, narrate, impress, and fill up space but never quite get to the point so that you end up going back to the beginning of the long confusing text and try to reread, but then you start wondering what's for dinner or what's on TV instead.

Yes, this book will also include some bad jokes.

This book is as small as possible because it leaves things out.

You're going to read that time and time again, but it's worth repeating: This book will leave things out.

We will focus on only the most important parts of WooCommerce so that you can understand them as easily as possible.

This book is not comprehensive. It does not contain everything you could know about WooCommerce. It contains only what a WooCommerce beginner needs to know.

THIS BOOK USES ALMOST NO CODE

You do not need to know any HTML and CSS to use this book. That is a deliberate decision because we want to make this book accessible to ordinary people. We believe you don't have to be a developer to use WooCommerce.

However, that will disappoint some of you because this book does not discuss designing major code changes to WooCommerce. If you do know CSS and PHP and want to dive into more advanced topics, there's a lot of advanced training at https://ostraining.com/classes.

THINGS IN THIS BOOK WILL CHANGE

WooCommerce will change, and you must learn to adapt as it changes. We believe that everything in this book is correct at the time of writing.

However, not only doesWooCommerce change, but so do the extra features and designs that you add on to it. As the book gets further away from its publication date, it's possible that some of the instructions and screen shots may become out of date.

One of the skills we teach you in this book is how to deal with changes inWooCommerce.

If you want to build modern websites, you must learn to accept and manage those changes. Please be patient with any changes you find.

Please contact us via books@ostraining.com if you find any changes. We'll update the book and send you a new copy.

WHAT YOU NEED FOR THIS BOOK

Now that you know a little bit about this book, let's make sure you're ready to follow along.

You need only three things to follow along with the exercises in this book:

1. A computer with an internet connection.
2. A web hosting account to install WordPress and WooCommerce.
3. The resources folder downloaded from http://ostra.in/ woo-resources.

Yes, that's really all you need.

Before you start, you probably need to know something about WooCommerce. Turn to Chapter 1, and let's get started.

ABOUT OSTRAINING

WooCommerce Explained is part of the OSTraining Book Club.

The Book Club gives you access to all of the "Explained" books from OSTraining:

- These books are always up-to-date. Because we self-publish, we can release constant updates.

- These books are active. We don't do long, boring explanations.

- You don't need any experience. The books are suitable even for complete beginners.

Join the OSTraining Book Club today: https://ostraining.com/books.

Use the coupon **"wcexplained"** to save 35% on your membership.

ABOUT NEXCESS

Magento 2 Explained was made possible by the support of Nexcess.net. Their Magento hosting is at https://www.nexcess.net/magento/hosting.

EXPERIENCE BEYOND.

New technology comes with a promise. Almost 20 years ago, from a small garage in Michigan, we set out to fulfill that promise: to become a hosting provider that empowers clients to create and grow the businesses they want.

Now, from our Michigan headquarters, we hold data centers around the world that offer the best in terms of performance, reliability, and control.

By embracing complexity, providing stability, and working with our clients, partners, and team members, we've managed to create innovations that have changed the face of web hosting support and management forever.

Experience the promise of technology with Nexcess.

TOGETHER WE CAN DO IT BETTER.

We've had over 17 years to polish our team and technology. We promise performance and support beyond what you've come to expect from the industry. We deliver on that promise by fine-tuning our performance-optimized infrastructure to your needs. Whether you're a Magento merchant, a growing enterprise, or a blogging fanatic, Nexcess Cloud solutions are built to help you outperform the competition. Your success is our success, let's grow and succeed together.

UNRIVALED SUPPORT

We're proud of what we do and love providing unmatched support 24 hours a day, 365 days a year. Our dedicated Support Team and Enterprise Support Group (ESG) work together to not only fix problems but to prevent them before they arise.

VETERANS IN ECOMMERCE

We currently manage and support more than 40,000 merchants around the globe. All benefit from an eCommerce-optimized infrastructure, designed to deliver unparalleled security, scalability, and performance.

SECURE AND RELIABLE PERFORMANCE

The Nexcess Cloud runs on a combination of optimized software and top-of-the-line hardware, all managed within our secure state-of-the-art data centers. Merchants expect and deserve reliable and rapid performance from their stores. Give your customers a seamless experience with eCommerce-optimized cloud hosting, and convert a great first impression into repeat business.

BEYOND SIMPLE MIGRATION

If you're considering changing hosts but are overwhelmed by the logistics of moving your site, leave it to us. Our dedicated migrations team will manage all the details of the move for you, with little to no downtime. If we require your input, we'll guide you every step of the way. No frustration, just seamless migration. We will:
- Transfer all site data.
- Synchronize database content.
- Assist with email issues or misdelivery.
- Arrange a time to change DNS information.

ABOUT THE OSTRAINING TEAM

Patrick Rauland is obsessed with WooCommerce. He's used it as a customer, worked for WooCommerce support, developed core functionality, led three releases, and helped plan their yearly conference. He now helps people by writing on his blog, his courses and books like this one. Patrick lives in Denver Colorado where you can probably find him at a local coffee shop typing away.

Stephen Burge has split his career between teaching and web development. In 2007, he combined the two by starting to teach web development. His company, OSTraining, now teaches people how to use the web's most popular software. Stephen is originally from England and now lives in Florida.

This book also would not be possible without the help of the OSTraining team.

Thanks to Dan Maynard and Topher DeRosia who worked on the video versions of this material.

Thanks to Sam Warburton who helped turn this material into a book.

Thanks to Stephen's wife, Stacey. She has saved him from many mistakes over the years, and many terrible typos in this book.

WE OFTEN UPDATE THIS BOOK

This is version 1.3 of WooCommerce Explained. This version was released on April 9, 2018.

We aim to keep this book up-to-date, and so regularly release new versions to keep up with changes in WordPress and WooCommerce.

If you find anything that is out-of-date, please email us at books@ostraining.com. We'll update the book, and to say thank you, we'll provide you with a new copy.

Thanks to Nina Breygin for reporting errors.

THINGS TO BE AWARE OF

We often release updates for this book. Most of the time, frequent updates are wonderful. If WooCommerce makes a change in the morning, we can have a new version of this book available in the afternoon. Most traditional publishers wait years and years before updating their books.

There are two disadvantages to be aware of:

- Page numbers do change. We often add and remove material from the book to reflect changes in WooCommerce.
- There's no index at the back of this book. This is because page numbers do change, and also because our self-publishing platform doesn't have a way to create indexes yet. We hope to find a solution for that soon.

Hopefully, you'll agree that the advantages outweigh the disadvantages. If you have any questions, we're always happy to chat: books@ostraining.com.

ARE YOU AN AUTHOR?

If you enjoy writing about the web, we'd love to talk with you.

Most publishing companies are slow, boring, inflexible, and don't pay very well.

Here at OSTraining, we try to be different:

- **Fun**: We use modern publishing tools that make writing books as easy as blogging.
- **Fast**: We move quickly. Some books get written and published in less than a month.
- **Flexible**: It's easy to update your books. If technology changes in the morning, you can update your book by the afternoon.
- **Fair**: Profits from the books are shared 50/50 with the author.

Do you have a topic you'd love to write about? We publish books on almost all web-related topics.

Whether you want to write a short 100-page overview, or a comprehensive 500-page guide, we'd love to hear from you.

Contact us via email: books@ostraining.com.

SPONSOR AN OSTRAINING BOOK

Is your company interested in sponsoring an OSTraining book?

Our books are some of the world's best-selling guides to the software they cover.

People love to read our books and learn about new web design topics.

Why not reach those people? Partner with us to showcase your company to thousands of web developers.

We have partnered with Acquia, Pantheon, Nexcess, GoDaddy, InMotion, GlowHost and Ecwid to provide sponsored training to millions of people.

If you want to learn more, visit https://marketing.ostraining.com or email us at books@ostraining.com.

WE WANT TO HEAR FROM YOU

Are you satisfied with your purchase of WooCommerce Explained? Let us know and help us reach others who would benefit from this book.

We encourage you to share your experience. Here are two ways you can help:

- Leave your review on Amazon's product page of WooCommerce Explained.
- Email your review to books@ostraining.com.

Thanks for reading WooCommerce Explained. We wish you the best in your future endeavors with WooCommerce.

ABOUT THE LEGAL DETAILS

WOOCOMMERCE EXPLAINED

PATRICK RAULAND

STEPHEN BURGE

OSTraining

CONTENTS

CHAPTER 1.

WOOCOMMERCE EXPLAINED

In this book, we're going to show you how to set up your own store with WooCommerce.

You'll see how to add features and make the store look beautiful. And, most importantly, we'll share common sense eCommerce tips so you'll learn how to make money from your store.

Before we start, let's give you some background information about WooCommerce. This chapter is a brief introduction to what WooCommerce is, where it came from, and who uses it.

WOOCOMMERCE IS BASED ON WORDPRESS

WooCommerce is a WordPress plugin, so you must have a WordPress site.

One of the great things about running your store on WooCommerce is that you control your own data. There are no rules and regulations about how you use it. And if you don't like how something works, you can update or customize it yourself. When you choose WooCommerce, you're choosing freedom, because nothing is out of bounds.

In addition, the main plugin is free. That means you don't have to pay any monthly fees to use it.

If you aren't familiar with WordPress, we do recommend you learn some basic WordPress skills. It will be a big help when you use WooCommerce. Try our "WordPress Explained" book: https://ostraining.com/books/wordpress/.

THE HISTORY OF WOOCOMMERCE

Here's some of the key information you should know about WooCommerce:

- **When did WooCommerce start?** WooCommerce launched in 2011 and was based on an existing shopping cart called Jigoshop.

- **Where did WooCommerce start?** It was created by an international team based out of South Africa. It now has developers based all over the world, with particularly strong representation coming from Europe, North America, Southeast Asia and of course, Australia.

- **Who runs WooCommerce?** WooComerce is developed by two different groups of people. One group works for Automattic, who are the owners of WooCommerce. The other group is volunteers; however, they do still need to keep a roof over their heads and eat. Many of these volunteers have WooCommerce businesses in the day-time and volunteer to keep the project growing.

WOOCOMMERCE IS POPULAR

If you choose WooCommerce, you will be using the most popular eCommerce platform on the web.

WooCommerce is capable of selling anything, whether it's physical products, digital products, or services.

Nearly 42% of all online store owners choose WooCommerce, according to BuiltWith. To see those statistics for yourself, visit https://trends.builtwith.com/shop and click "The Entire Internet" in the right sidebar.

WHO USES WOOCOMMERCE?

Let's give you an overview of some of the different organizations that use WooCommerce to sell things online.

Large companies: Many famous organizations use WooCommerce. One prominent example is Duracell, who use WooCommerce to sell lighting, batteries and solar lighting at http://duracelllighting.com.

Attractions: Many tourism locations and entertainment venues rely on WooCommerce. Ripley's Believe it or Not uses WooCommerce for many tasks, including their book and DVD store: http://ripleys.com/books.

Sports teams: The All Blacks are the national rugby team of New Zealand and are the most famous rugby team in the world.

They use WooCommerce to sell accessories and clothing: https://allblackshop.com.

Magazines: Kinfolk is a slow lifestyle magazine that aims to promote quality of life. They use WooCommerce to sell magazine subscriptions at https://kinfolk.com/shop.

You can find more great examples of WooCommerce sites at https://woocommerce.com/showcase.

IS WOOCOMMERCE FREE?

Technically it's *freemium*. That means that some of the functionality is free and some of it is a paid upgrade.

One of the great things about WooCommerce is that the core is free. The free version comes with several payment gateways and also basic shipping options, so it's possible to set up a basic store at no cost.

There are also free and commercial extensions you can use to add more features to your store.

One example of a free extension is the WooCommerce Stripe Payment Gateway. You can download this plugin from WordPress.org, and it will allow your customers to pay with Stripe: http://ostra.in/woo-stripe. We'll show you how to download and install this plugin in the chapter called, "Installing WooCommerce Explained".

In contrast, if you want your customers to pay with Authorize.net, there's a plugin available for $79 at http://ostra.in/woo-auth. There are plenty of other premium extensions, like memberships and automated recurring payments. Most of the commercial plugins cost between $50 and $200.

WOOCOMMERCE CUSTOMER PAYMENT OPTIONS

WooCommerce comes preinstalled with four payment gateways:

- Direct bank transfer
- Cheque payment
- Cash on delivery
- PayPal

If you need more options, there are over 110 different payment plugins available via http://ostra.in/woo-pay.

stripe

Accept Visa, MasterCard, American Express, Discover, JCB, and Diners Club cards directly on your store.

FROM: Free! >

amazon pay

Amazon Pay is embedded in your WooCommerce store. Transactions take place via Amazon widgets, so the buyer never leaves your site.

FROM: Free! >

PayFast

Take payments on your WooCommerce store via PayFast (redirect method).

FROM: Free! >

Authorize.Net AIM

Take credit card payments direct on your checkout using the Authorize.net (AIM) payment gateway for WooCommerce.

FROM: $79.00 >

PayPal Pro

Take credit card payments directly on your checkout using PayPal Pro.

FROM: $79.00 >

Authorize.Net
a CyberSource solution

Authorize CIM gateway with support for pre-orders and subscriptions.

FROM: $79.00 >

WOOCOMMERCE AND THEMES

There are hundreds of thousands of WordPress themes available, but not all of them will work with WooCommerce.

Before choosing a theme for your store, I highly recommend that you check to see if it's compatible with WooCommerce. If it's not clear on the download or sales page, definitely contact the theme developer.

Some elements of WooCommerce do need unique styles, and not every theme is WooCommerce-friendly.

The WooCommerce team offers a free theme called Storefront that is completely designed with WooCommerce sites in mind: https://woocommerce.com/storefront. We're going to be using Storefront throughout this book.

Storefront is an *intuitive* & *flexible*, **free** WordPress theme offering deep integration with WooCommerce.

It's the perfect platform for your next WooCommerce project.

10 OTHER THINGS THAT WOOCOMMERCE OFFERS

1. **Security:** The WooCommerce code is audited by Sucuri, which is an industry leader in plugin security. When dealing with e-commerce, you are dealing with both your own money and with other people's money. That's a serious responsibility. You're making a good choice with WooCommerce, but there are things you must do to keep your site safe, and we'll cover those in the chapter, "WooCommerce Security Explained".

2. **A large community of developers**. Many of the WooCommerce extensions are not built by the WooCommerce team but rather are built by third-party developers. WooCommerce has made it very easy to build add-ons and extensions for WooCommerce. So, people create these extensions and then sell them to people like you.

3. **Shipping**: WooCommerce offers you a plethora of options when it comes to shipping. From the basic (free shipping and flat rate shipping) to the more complex (live rates provided by USPS). You as a store owner can choose which

is right for your customer. We'll cover shipping in the chapter, "WooCommerce Shipping Explained".

4. **Taxes**: WooCommerce tries very hard to make taxes easy to digest, but you will need to do some research about the requirements where you live. Do you charge the tax required where the customer is located or where you are? If you are selling in Europe, do you have to use the new VAT MOSS system? Find out more in the chapter, "WooCommerce Taxes Explained".

5. **SEO**: WordPress has plugins to make your site SEO-friendly, and these plugins work for WooCommerce too. We'll show you how to optimize your store in the chapter, "WooCommerce SEO Explained".

6. **Coupons**: By default, WooCommerce allows you to create coupons and discounts for your customers, and you'll learn how to use these in the chapter, "WooCommerce Coupons Explained".

7. **Reporting and analytics**: These are incredibly important in any e-commerce store. You need to know how many sales you've had, how much money you've brought in and perhaps how much money you have lost due to fraud and things like that. WooCommerce not only comes with some built-in reporting, but there are also some excellent extensions to get you even more data about what's happening throughout your store. Find out how to use this data in "WooCommerce Reports Explained".

8. **Customer management**: You need to know who purchased from you, what they purchased, how often they purchase, where they live and other things like that. WooCommerce offers this as part of the core, and we explain more about customer management in "WooCommerce Order Management Explained".

9. **Support**: There is a free, community support forum on WordPress.org at https://wordpress.org/support/plugin/

woocommerce. They don't offer customization on their products, but they will try to help you if you have questions.

10. **Documentation**: WooCommerce comes with excellent documentation at https://docs.woocommerce.com.

WHAT'S NEXT?

Now that you know some of the background behind WooCommerce, we're going to help you get familiar with the platform.

Together we'll tour the official demo site and show you many of the important features in WooCommerce.

Turn the page, and let's begin!

CHAPTER 2.

TOURING A WOOCOMMERCE SITE EXPLAINED

One of the best ways to get familiar with WooCommerce is to take a close look at a professionally-created installation.

In this chapter, we are going to take a look at some of the features of WooCommerce in action.

We're going to take a look at the demo of WooCommerce available at https://demo.woothemes.com/storefront. Storefront is the official WooCommerce theme. It is built and maintained by WooCommerce core developers. Storefront is available for free, but it is not required for WooCommerce. You can use any theme that you want.

The image below shows what you'll see when you visit https://demo.woothemes.com/storefront. The homepage is dominated by a large video playing in the background.

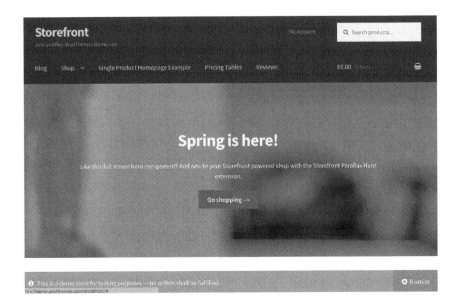

Let's get started with our tour.

We're going to use the black admin bar, shown in the image below, for this tour. These five links contain many of the important things you need to know about WooCommerce.

THE BLOG LINK

- Click the "Blog" link, and you'll see a traditional WordPress blog layout.

This page is a reminder that WooCommerce is 100% integrated with WordPress. You can have your blog and your store in the same place. This saves you a ton of time when it comes to analyzing your Google Analytics reports. It's *so* much easier if everything is on one domain instead of one domain for your blog and another for your store.

Posted on September 1, 2014

Birds In Flight And The Power Of A Remote Working Team

Written by
Sentient User

Posted in
Business, General

Comments
Leave a comment

Do you remember the first time you took note of a flock of birds slipstreaming? And someone explained the way they fly aerodynamically and take turns to head up the V-shape and be carried along by the strength of their fellows? Nature is smart. We can learn a lot from it.

THE SHOP LINK

- Hover over the "Shop" link, and you'll see a massive dropdown menu with lots of product categories, as shown below.

- Click the "Shop" link at the top-level of the menu, and you'll go to this page https://demo.woothemes.com/storefront/shop/.

- You'll now see the main WooCommerce shop page, as in the image below. The scuba tank is the central, featured product on the site.

- Try clicking the "Add to cart" button for the scuba tank, as shown below.

Shop

Cart

No products in the cart

Product Categories

☐ Clothing
☐ Bags
☐ Blouses
☐ Dresses
☐ Footwear
☐ Hats
☐ Hoodies
☐ Shirts
☐ Skirts
☐ T-shirts

- You'll see that the scuba tank is instantly added to your cart:

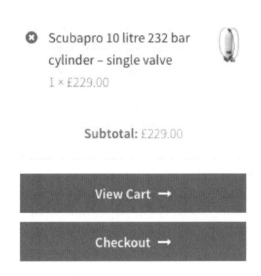

Cart

- Your cart is also available in the black admin bar:

- Further down the "Shop" page, you can see a large grid of products. These products are sorted by "newness" so the top row shows the last three products added to the site:

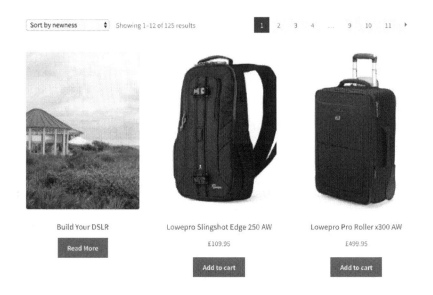

Sort by newness ⇅ Showing 1–12 of 125 results   1 2 3 4 ... 9 10 11 ▶

Build Your DSLR

Read More

Lowepro Slingshot Edge 250 AW

£109.95

Add to cart

Lowepro Pro Roller x300 AW

£499.95

Add to cart

- In the right-sidebar, you can see ways to search for products. You can see product categories:

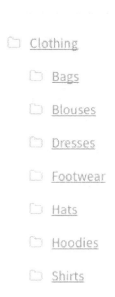

Product Categories

🗀 Clothing

🗀 Bags

🗀 Blouses

🗀 Dresses

🗀 Footwear

🗀 Hats

🗀 Hoodies

🗀 Shirts

- You can also drill down and search for products by price and color:

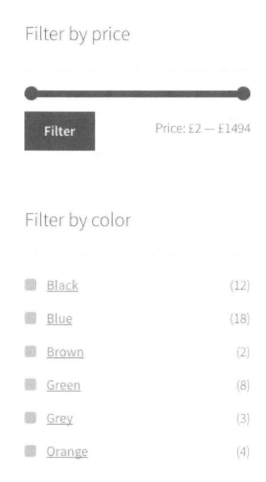

Filter by price

Filter   Price: £2 — £1494

Filter by color

Black   (12)

Blue   (18)

Brown   (2)

Green   (8)

Grey   (3)

Orange   (4)

- Click on the "More details" link for the scuba tank, as shown in the image below.

Shop

- You'll now see a standard WooCommerce product layout, as shown in the image below.

There's a nice, large image, which you can enlarge if you click it. We also have a title, the price, a short description, and some areas at the bottom for a longer description and reviews.

Scubapro 10 litre 232 bar cylinder – single valve

£229.00

10 Litre 232 Bar Cylinder with single outlet valve from Scubapro. Includes tank boot but the tank carry handle is not included and is shown for illustration purposes only.

Pellentesque habitant morbi tristique senectus et netus et malesuada fames ac turpis egestas. Vestibulum tortor quam, feugiat vitae, ultricies eget, tempor sit amet, ante. Donec eu libero sit amet quam egestas semper. Aenean ultricies mi vitae est. Mauris placerat eleifend leo.

| 1 | Add to cart |

Category: Scuba gear

Description   >

Reviews (0)

Product Description

10 Litre 232 Bar Cylinder with single outlet valve from Scubapro. Includes tank boot but the tank carry handle is not included and is shown for illustration purposes only.

This is a very simple product. The reason for this is because there's only one kind of scuba tank. However, WooCommerce can handle more complex products with more options.

- Go to "Shop" and then click "Blouses".

- You'll see the page shows an overview of all the products in a single category.
- By default the products are sorted by newness, but you can change that sorting option, as you can see in the image below.

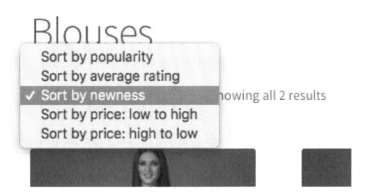

- You'll notice that these products don't have "Add to cart" buttons. Instead, they have "Select options" buttons.
- Click on one of the "Select options" buttons.

Blouses

Sort by newness ⬍   Showing all 2 results

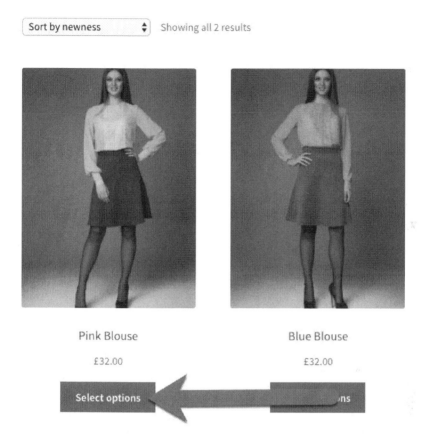

Pink Blouse	Blue Blouse
£32.00	£32.00

Select options ⬅ ns

Notice that for these products, you can choose a color and a size.

The cost of the "Pink Blouse" doesn't change if you choose different options, but many products will have different prices for different options. The "Add to Cart" button will only become active after you've chosen some options.

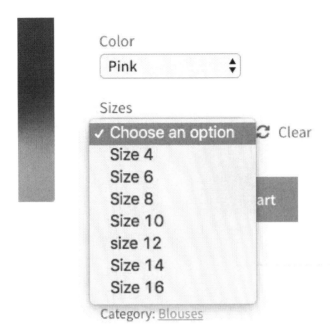

Color

Pink ↕

Sizes

✓ Choose an option   ⟳ Clear
Size 4
Size 6
Size 8   art
Size 10
size 12
Size 14
Size 16

Category: Blouses

- Underneath the main product description, you'll also see "Related Products".

Related products are shown to increase sales dramatically. These products are manually chosen by the person who created the store. Sometimes the choice is easy. In this case, the "Pink Blouse" is related to the "Blue Blouse".

Related Products

Blue Blouse

£32.00

Select options

- If we click on "Select options," or if we click on the photo, it takes us to another product page. So, we can go from one product related product to another. Let's stay on the pink blouse page.

- Click "Add to Cart" for the product you're viewing, and you'll see this green message bar:

- You'll see several "View Cart" buttons on the page.
- Click on one of these buttons, and you'll see what's in your shopping cart.
- On this screen, as shown in the image below, we have the option of changing the quantity or removing the item from our cart. We could also apply a coupon code here.

Cart

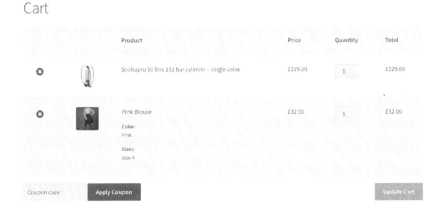

- Click the "Proceed to Checkout" button in the bottom-right corner, as shown below.

Cart Totals

Subtotal	£261.00
Total	£261.00

Proceed to Checkout →

- You will now see the final page in the checkout process. You will be required to put in all the normal information when you buy something online.

Checkout

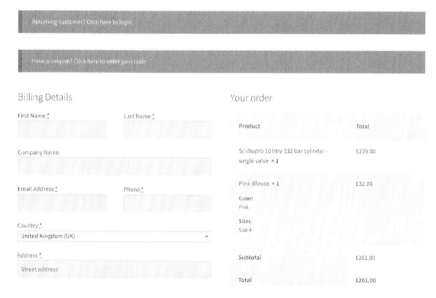

Returning customer? Click here to login

Have a coupon? Click here to enter your code

Billing Details

First Name *   Last Name *

Company Name

Email Address *   Phone *

Country *
United Kingdom (UK)

Address *
Street address

Your order

Product	Total
Scubapro 10 litre 232 bar cylinder – single valve × 1	£229.00
Pink Blouse × 1	£32.00
Color: Pink	
Sizes: Size 4	
Subtotal	£261.00
Total	£261.00

- If you do complete this page successfully, you'll see an "Order Received" page. Sorry, but don't expect your scuba tank and your blouse to arrive any time soon.

Order Received

Thank you. Your order has been received.

ORDER NUMBER:
9904

DATE:
June 5, 2017

TOTAL:
£261.00

PAYMENT METHOD:
Check Payments

Please send a check to Store Name, Store Street, Store Town, Store State / County, Store Postcode.

THE SINGLE PRODUCT HOMEPAGE LINK

- Click "Single Product Homepage Example" in the main menu.
- You'll see that this is a large series of images, which are designed to sell a single product.

If you don't have a large store, or if you have one or two very important products, you can create layouts like this to focus your customer's attention.

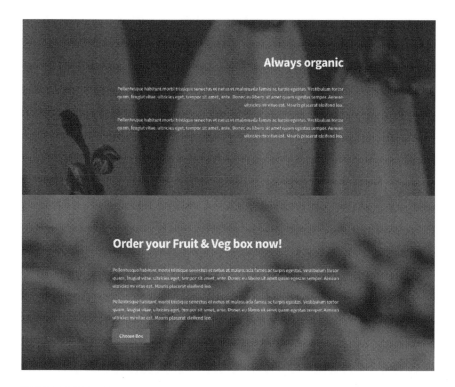

THE PRICING TABLES LINK

- Click "Pricing Tables" in the main menu.
- You'll now see a table with three options.

This page displays the different features available to different levels of membership and the prices. This shows that you can use WooCommerce to sell single products, but also memberships and subscriptions.

Pricing Tables

Bronze Membership	Silver Membership	Gold Membership
Here's a bronze level feature	Here's a silver level feature	Here's a gold level feature
Here's another bronze level feature	Here's another silver level feature	Here's another gold level feature
Here's another bronze level feature	Here's another silver level feature	Here's another gold level feature
Here's another bronze level feature	Here's another silver level feature	Here's another gold level feature
£10.00	£25.00	£50.00
Add to cart	Add to cart	Add to cart

THE REVIEWS LINK

- Click "Reviews" in the main menu. You'll see sample reviews for some of the dummy products, as shown on the screen below.

- Notice the green bar across the top of the screen. The "Storefront Reviews" text links to this page: https://woocommerce.com/products/storefront-reviews/.

Reviews

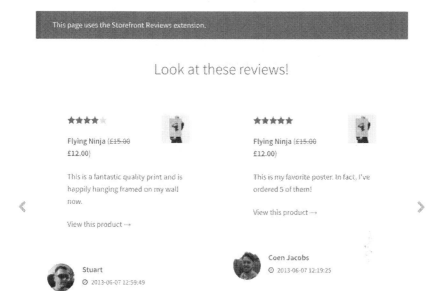

WooCommerce has a lot of great, free features, but there are also many paid extensions. Some of these extensions are relatively cheap. For example, the "Storefront Reviews" extension is $19 per year for a single site. However, some more complex extensions can cost hundreds of dollars per year. You can find a full list of WooCommerce extensions at http://ostra.in/woo-ext.

WHAT'S NEXT?

This chapter gave you a visual introduction to WooCommerce. Until you become more experienced with WooCommerce, your store will look very similar to this demo. We're going to be using the Storefront theme throughout much of this book.

Now that you know what WooCommerce looks like and have seen some of its features, it's time to move on and start using WooCommerce. In the next chapter, we'll walk you through installing your first WooCommerce site.

CHAPTER 3.

INSTALLING WOOCOMMERCE EXPLAINED

In this chapter, we're going to take you through the WooCommerce installation and setup.

Normally, installing WooCommerce is a two part process. First, you install WordPress, and then you install WooCommerce as a plugin.

However, there are some exceptions to this process. For example, if you sign up for some hosting companies and tell them you want to use WooCommerce, they will install WordPress and WooCommerce together for you.

Not all parts of this chapter will be relevant for all of you. Where you go next depends on whether you have a site ready to use when following along with this book:

- If you already have a WordPress site with WooCommerce installed: you can skip this chapter entirely.

- If you already have a WordPress site installed but without WooCommerce: go to the "How to Install WooCommerce" section of this chapter.

- If you don't have a WordPress site yet, keep reading!

HOW TO INSTALL WORDPRESS ON A WEB SERVER

There are two common options for hosting a WordPress and WooCommerce site. You can host your site on:

- A web server
- A local server on your computer

Choosing the best place to install your site is important, so here is an explanation of the difference between the two options.

Hosting your site on a web server has some significant advantages:

- You can access it from anywhere.
- You can easily share the site with other people if you have questions or get stuck.
- When you're ready to launch your site, your site is already in the perfect location.

The only real disadvantage to using a web server is that it's likely to cost you a few dollars a month.

You will need to choose a hosting company that uses PHP and MySQL. You need PHP because that is the language WordPress and WooCommerce are written in. You need MySQL because it is the type of database normally used with WooCommerce. These are the minimum versions recommended:

- **PHP:** 5.6
- **MySQL:** 5.6 or above

Most hosting companies now support WordPress and WooCommerce, but it's worth choosing carefully. Some hosting companies are much better than others.

Here is some advice before picking your host:

- Search https://wordpress.org/support/ for other people's experiences with that host.

- Contact the hosting company's customer support and ask what it knows about WooCommerce. One of our training students actually called the phone numbers of several hosts and evaluated their response. After all, in an emergency you don't want to be on hold for an hour or to be talking to someone who knows nothing about WooCommerce.

You can install WooCommerce on almost any server that has PHP and MySQL installed. However, there are hosting companies that specialize in WordPress and some that specialize in WooCommerce.

There are many advantages to choosing WooCommerce-specific hosting services:

- They are managed by WooCommerce experts who know exactly what WordPress and WooCommerce sites need to run well.

- They can keep your web server up to date, which greatly increases security.

- They provide extra features that make it easier to install and manage WordPress and WooCommerce sites.

If you want to install WordPress on a server yourself, you can find instructions at http://ostraining.com/books/woocommerce/web.

We highly recommend http://nexcess.net as a company that really knows what they're doing with WooCommerce. They offer great hosting, excellent support, and a ton of extra services.

If you choose Nexcess, this guide will take you through the process of getting your WooCommerce site up-and-running.

Nexcess have details of their WooCommerce hosting at https://nexcess.net/woocommerce/hosting. Start your sign-up process by visiting this page. You'll see three different plan options. The plan you choose will depend on the size of your site. SIP 100 is a good plan for a new site.

- Click the "Sign Up" button next to the plan you want.

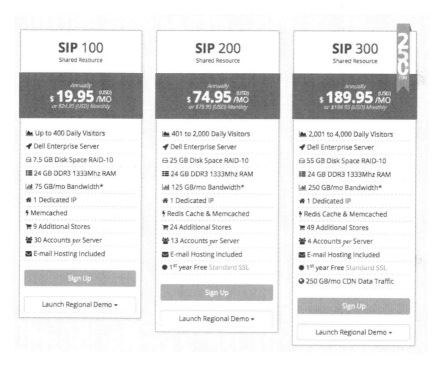

You'll be taken to the Nexcess checkout process. On the first screen you can choose from several options:

- **Term**: Sign up on a monthly or annual basis.
- **Server Location**: Nexcess offers server locations in the US, the UK, Australia, and the Netherlands.

- **Your Domain**: You can use your own domain name or buy one from Nexcess.

Click the "Add to Cart" button when you've chosen from these options.

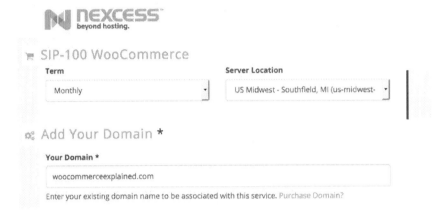

- You'll now see an overview of your plan and domain name. Click the green "Checkout" button if these details are correct.

Now it's time to sign up for a Nexcess account.

- On the next screen, click "New to Nexcess? Sign Up".

Sign In

Email

user@example.com

Password

Reset Password

New to Nexcess? Sign Up

LOGIN

- Nexcess will now ask you to create an email and password:

Sign Up

Already have an account? Sign In

Email

info@ostraining.com

Password

•••••••••••••••••••••••••••••

Confirm Password

•••••••••••••••••••••••••••••

By signing up, you agree to our Terms of Service & Acceptable Use Policy

SIGN UP

- You'll see the Thank You message in the image below. The text of the message will change based on the payment option you choose.

Thank You For Your Order!

Your order number(s): **51690**

To complete the process, please log in to PayPal to complete payment.

You will receive a confirmation e-mail in just a few minutes and we will begin processing your order as soon as you have sent payment via PayPal. We may contact you with questions should they arise so sit tight and thanks again for choosing Nexcess!

- Check your email inbox. Nexcess will send you an email with details of your new WooCommerce site. The email will contain a link to your WooCommerce site, plus the username and password.

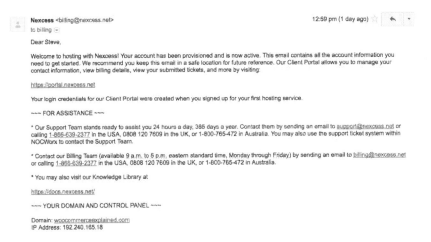

- Clink the link in your email to visit your new site.

- Use the login details to log into the site.

- You'll be redirected to the WooCommerce setup page. You can now go to the "How to Install WooCommerce in a WordPress site" section of this book and follow along with the WooCommerce set-up instructions.

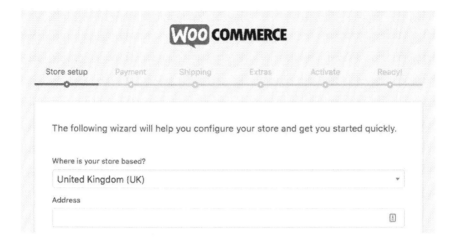

HOW TO INSTALL WORDPRESS ON YOUR COMPUTER

There are some advantages to installing WordPress and WooCommerce on your computer. However, we do not recommend this option for beginners.

It can be tempting to choose to have WordPress on your computer. Advanced users do find several useful advantages to this choice:

- **Working offline:** You can work without an Internet connection.

- **Privacy:** Your site will be safe and private, accessible only to people who can access that computer.

- **Free:** There are no fees to pay.

- **Fast**: You don't need to connect to a remote server.

However, there are also several important disadvantages to using a computer:

- **Extra installations needed:** You need to download and configure special software for your computer.

- **Difficult to get help:** You can't easily show it to other people and ask for help.

- **Only one computer:** You can access it only from the computer you used to install it.

- **Need to move to launch:** When you're ready to make your site public, you need to move everything to a web server and adjust for any differences between the two locations. Moving a WordPress site is not easy for beginners.

Because of these disadvantages, installing on your computer can present significant obstacles for a beginner. Do not take this route until you have more experience.

However, if you do feel comfortable overcoming these obstacles, you can find instructions on how to install WordPress on your computer at http://ostraining.com/books/woocommerce/local.

HOW TO INSTALL WOOCOMMERCE IN A WORDPRESS SITE

Installing WooCommerce is a little different from installing most WordPress plugins.

WooCommerce has a complete onboarding process to guide you through the set-up of your site. WooCommerce will ask you a series of questions, which allows you to customize your payment, shipping, tax and other options.

Let's walk through the WooCommerce installation process.

- Log into your WordPress site.

- From the left-side menu, go to "Plugins" and then "Add New":

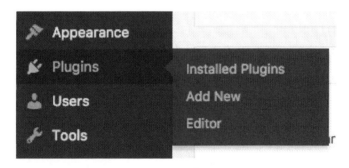

- Type "woocommerce" into the search box in the top-right corner, as shown below.

- Click "Install Now" next to WooCommerce. You may notice that we searched only for "WooCommerce" and it found 5,000 plugins. This is a *really* popular plugin!

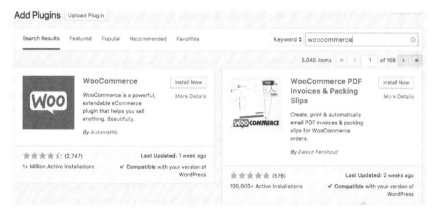

- The "Install Now" button will change to a blue "Activate" button.

- Click "Activate".

- You'll now be taken to the WooCommerce onboarding wizard, which looks like the image below.

- Fill out your store's address – or your home office if you don't have a brick and mortar store.

- Choose your currency and what type of products you sell (digital or physical).

- At the bottom of the screen, there's a checkbox allowing WooCommerce to collect non-sensitive information about your store. If you leave this checked, your site will send WooCommerce information to make their software better.

- Click the purple "Let's go!" button to continue.

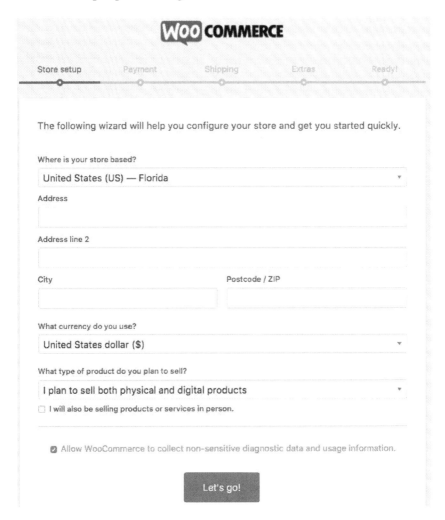

On the next screen, you can choose how you want to get paid. WooCommerce offers a few options you can configure right now, and there are hundreds you can configure later.

WooCommerce presents two options (and offline payments like accepting checks):

- **Stripe**: http://ostra.in/woo-stripe
- **PayPal**: http://ostra.in/woo-paypal

These options might look pretty similar to someone who is just getting started. Let me try to simplify this for you:

- **Stripe** let's you accept credit cards.
- **PayPal** lets you accept credit cards and also PayPal payments.

For new store owners, I recommend using both Stripe and PayPal. I've used Stripe for years and I love their customer service, pricing, and their interface, so I'm definitely going to use Stripe with this site.

- The toggle for Stripe should already be set to "on" (purple). If you don't already have a Stripe account, you can check the box to automatically create an account for you.
- Make sure the toggle for PayPal is also on.
- Click "Continue" to move on to the next step.

Note: Depending on your location you may see different payment options here. Ex. Stripe isn't available in all countries, so you may not see Stripe if you're not in a supported country. If that's the case, click the link for "Additional payment methods" to find a gateway you can use. You can do this after you finish the setup.

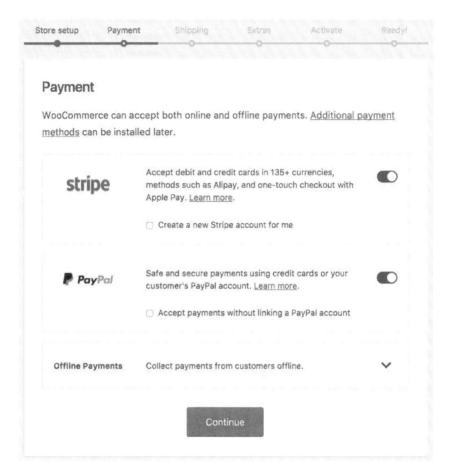

The next screen is all about Shipping. You'll only see this screen if you are selling physical products. So if you selected "Digital Products" on the first screen, you'll skip this step.

You'll be prompted about *how* you want to ship your products. If you are based in the United States, you'll see "Live Rates" as the default method. That means your customers can choose a rate from USPS at checkout, and you as the store owner don't have to guesstimate a shipping cost. It's automatically calculated, and you can even print out a label at home. It's a *huge* time saver. Thus, I strongly recommend using live rates.

Note: If you select "Live Rates," WooCommerce will download the Jetpack plugin and install it for you automatically. Jetpack helps manage your connection to WordPress.com that provides this free service.

If you don't want to use Live Rates, or you don't live in the United States, you can select "Flat Rate" or "Free" – and for Flat Rate, you can enter your rate.

You'll also be prompted to select shipping units. These are determined by your location, so you most likely won't have to change this. WooCommerce correctly assumed I want to use ounces and inches for my store.

• Click "Continue" when you're done.

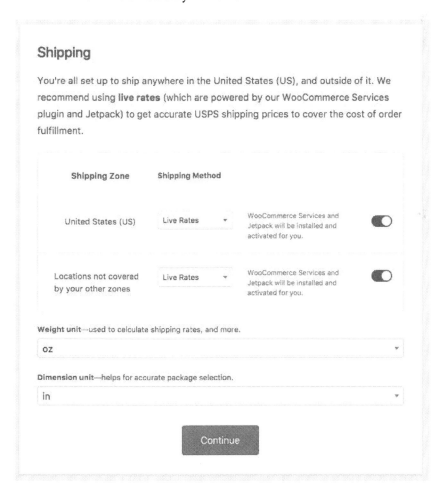

On the next page, you can enable two things, both of which I recommend.

- **Storefront Theme:** This is the recommended WooCommerce theme and is a great default theme. You can do a lot of customization with it, which we'll explore later in this book. You can always switch at a later time to a different theme if you don't like Storefront.

- **Automated Taxes:** These are a huge deal for store owners. You want to get your store online and start making sales. You don't want to be fiddling with tax rates.

If you are using Live Rates for shipping, you already have all of the infrastructure in place. You can just turn on Automated Taxes and save yourself a lot of time.

- Click "Continue" when you're done.

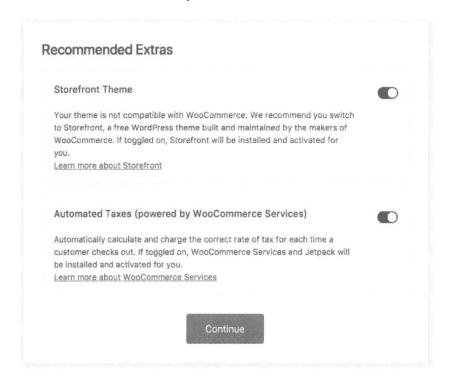

We're going to use a lot of free functionality from Jetpack including live shipping rates and automated taxes. To do that we have to connect our store to install Jetpack and then use Jetpack to connect our site to WordPress.com, which is the site running all of these free services.

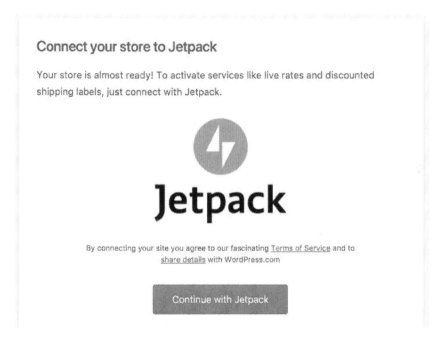

- Click "Continue with Jetpack".

Note: Some hosting settings prevent plugins from installing other plugins. If that happens, you'll see an error about not being able to install Jetpack. If that is the case, you can manually install it later via the Plugins menu.

This will take you to WordPress.com, and you'll have to authorize your site.

And we're done! Your store is now ready. That was the hardest part of setting up your store. Now our store is ready and we can create our first product.

- Click "Create a product" to continue on to the next step.

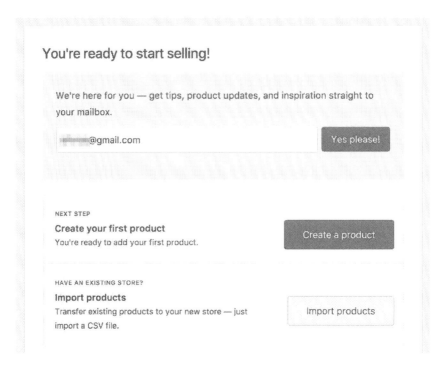

WHAT'S NEXT?

Congratulations! You now have a working e-commerce store using WordPress and WooCommerce.

In the next chapter, we'll create your first product and publish it on your site.

CHAPTER 4.

YOUR FIRST WOOCOMMERCE PRODUCT EXPLAINED

If you haven't noticed yet, WooCommerce *loves* purple. Since we're making a book about WooCommerce, we thought we'd make a store called **Purpleville** that sells only purple items.

We're going to sell some simple products and some complex products, all of which are designed to show off different features within WooCommerce.

The last step in the onboarding wizard is to create a product. We're going to do that now. And we're going to add our first product to our store.

- If you haven't done so already, click "Create a product".

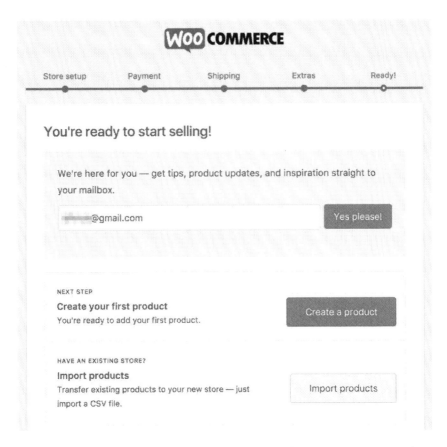

After installation, you will immediately see quite a few WooCommerce notifications.

- Dismiss the notifications about new features. You can also dismiss the notice about setting up Storefront. We'll do that later in this book.

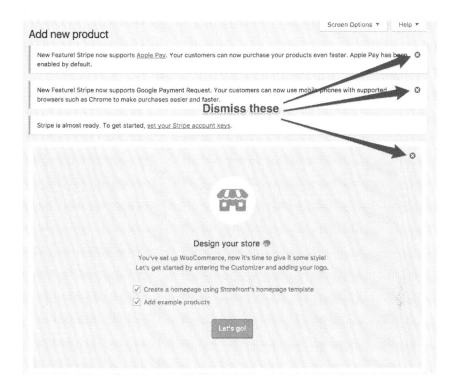

ADDING A NEW PRODUCT

After you dismiss all of these notices, you will see the "Add new product" page, as shown below.

Our first product is going to be a t-shirt.

- In the Title field, type in the name of the product: **Dinosaurs Are Awesome T-Shirt.**
- After you click out of the Title field, notice that WordPress has generated a product URL. This URL contains our product name. These are called Permalinks in the WordPress world. If you do want to make a cleaner URL, click the "Edit" button next to the URL and remove the "are-" text.

- You'll see your edited permalink, as shown in the screen below.
- Next, write in a description of the product.

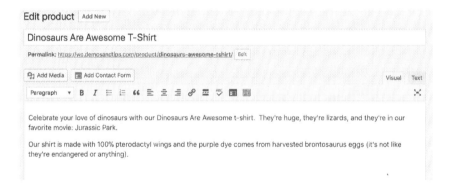

EXPLORING THE PRODUCT DATA SECTION

Below this Title and Description section, you'll see the "Product data" area. Here we can choose from a number of product types, such as simple products, grouped products, external/affiliate products and variable products.

For our example, we'll leave it as a simple product. Our product won't be virtual or downloadable – these are options that we'll cover in more detail later in the book.

- Set the "Regular price" to 30.
- Set the "Sale price" to 25.

On the left-hand side of this area, you'll see several tabs. Click through to explore these options:

- **Inventory**: This is where you can enter the SKU number and tell WooCommerce whether or not this product is in stock.

- **Shipping**: Here we can choose the weight of the product. You'll need to fill in the weight and dimensions if you want live shipping rates. Go ahead and enter something in here so we can see the live rates in action on the front end of our site.

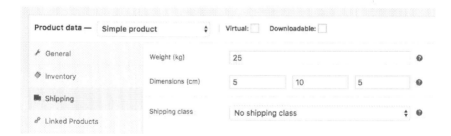

- **Linked Products**: Here we can link this Dinosaur T-Shirt to other products, in the hope of encouraging people to buy more products or higher-priced products. However, since this is our first product, we can't test this option yet.

- **Attributes**: If this Dinosaur T-Shirt came in different colors, we could use attributes and variations to display that to the user. We'll talk about these in the chapter called "WooCommerce Attributes and Variations Explained".

- **Advanced**: Here we can include a purchase note, a menu order, or disable reviews for the product.

ADDING A PRODUCT SHORT DESCRIPTION

Below this we have the "Product short description". The short description is a slightly briefer version of your description that is always displayed. The full description is often hidden behind a tab on the product page.

- Enter a short description of your product.

ADDING PRODUCT CATEGORIES AND TAGS

These categories and tags are ways in which we can categorize and organize our products.

In the right column, we have "Product categories". Let's create a "Clothing" category for our T-Shirt.

- Click "+ Add new category".

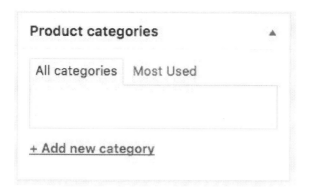

- Type in "Clothing" and then click "Add new category".

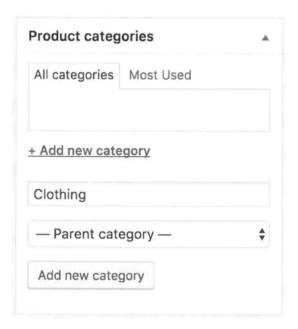

We can also add tags to our product, which work exactly like WordPress tags. Let's create a dinosaur tag so users can browse by dinosaur (how cool is that?).

- Type in the name of your tag into the field and click "Add".

ADDING A FEATURED IMAGE

And just like WordPress posts, we can add a Featured Image to our product. However, they're called "Product Image" when you place them on a product page.

- Scroll down until you see "Product image".

- Click "Set product image".

- Open the Resources folder that you can download from http://ostra.in/woo-resources. Upload the file called "dinosaurs-are-awesome.jpg". After uploading the image, your screen will look like this:

- Click the "Set product image" button in the bottom right corner.

- Your new T-Shirt image will now appear in the right sidebar of your screen:

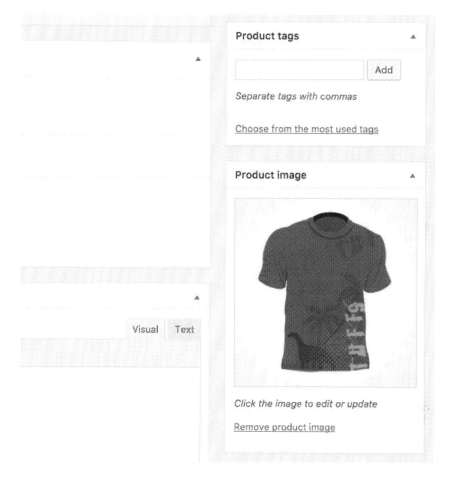

PUBLISHING THE PRODUCT

Let's publish the T-Shirt using the details we've entered so far.

- Scroll back to the top of the page and click the blue "Publish" button.

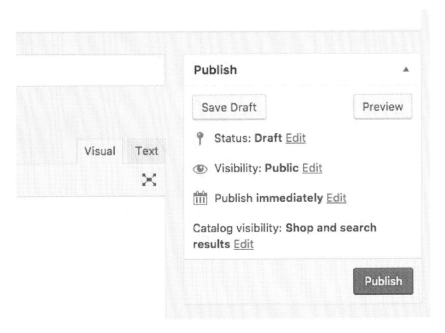

- Now go to the front of your site to view your new product. You'll see a screen similar to the one below.

As you can see, we have the product title, price, short description, product image, and the "Add to cart" button.

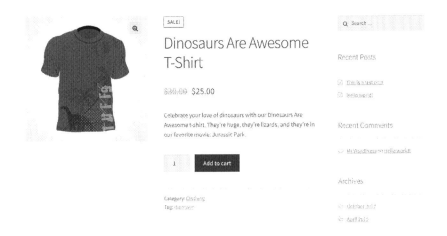

Below this, we see our long description and tabs for "Additional information" and "Reviews".

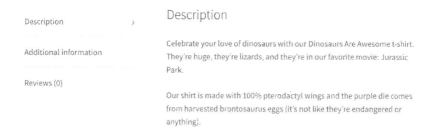

Description

Celebrate your love of dinosaurs with our Dinosaurs Are Awesome t-shirt. They're huge, they're lizards, and they're in our favorite movie: Jurassic Park.

Our shirt is made with 100% pterodactyl wings and the purple die comes from harvested brontosaurus eggs (it's not like they're endangered or anything).

- Click the "Additional information" link in the left sidebar.
- Here you'll see the weight and dimensions we set (assuming you set them). Once we enter attributes, you'll see attributes show up here as well.

Additional information

| Weight | 12 oz |
| Dimensions | 6 x 6 x 12 in |

That is how you create a product in WooCommerce. There were a few features not available to us because we haven't entered any other products or created any settings, such as shipping classes. In the future, we might need to come back and edit this product.

Overall, the experience is straightforward, especially if you're familiar with the WordPress Post Editor.

WHAT'S NEXT?

Now that our first product is ready, you can repeat this process to add more of your products.

We have at least one product in our store now, so let's allow people to buy a Dinosaur T-Shirt. In the next chapter, we'll connect WooCommerce to a payment gateway so we can start accepting credit cards and making some money!

CHAPTER 5.

WOOCOMMERCE CHECKOUT EXPLAINED

In this chapter, we are going to take a look at the checkout process.

We will go through the checkout from beginning to end, seeing what the customer sees. We are going to use Stripe and Paypal for our payment gateways.

SETTING UP STRIPE

If you decided to set up Stripe manually, like we did during the chapter called "Installing WooCommerce Explained," you will see this message inside your WordPress site:

> Stripe is almost ready. To get started, set your Stripe account keys.

Let's get rid of this message and configure our Stripe settings.

- We can click on the link in this message. That will take us directly to the Stripe settings page. You can also get to any of the checkout settings by going to "WooCommerce" and then "Settings".

- You'll be taken to a screen with a variety of tabs, as seen in the image below. Note that you may see more tabs if you have other WooCommerce extensions installed.

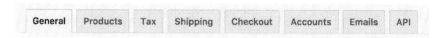

- Click on the "Checkout" tab.

Before we move on to Stripe settings, we want to make sure any credit card numbers entered on our site are secure. We can do that by forcing the user to load our checkout in HTTPS. That S at the end of HTTPS stands for secure. It encrypts all traffic so someone at the coffee shop can't intercept your customer's credit card. To load a page with HTTPS, you need an SSL certificate installed by your host.

This used to be an expensive process, but with the introduction of Let's Encrypt (https://letsencrypt.org), your host should be able to install an SSL certificate for you in a matter of minutes for free.

In the chapter called, "Installing WooCommerce Explained," we recommended against installing WooCommerce on your computer. The SSL certificate is one of the reasons why. It's very difficult to get an SSL certificate established to test your checkout.

- If you have an SSL certificate ready for your site, enable the "Force secure checkout" setting.

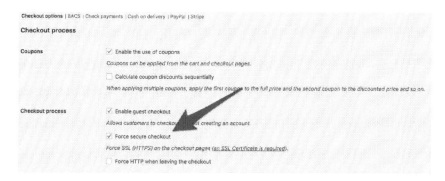

- Click "Save changes" at the bottom of the page.

- Now click "Stripe" on the top menu, as shown on the far right in the image below.

Checkout options | BACS | Check payments | Cash on delivery | PayPal | Stripe

- Now we can finally enter the credentials and get rid of that nag. We can also customize the settings to our needs.

- After you've entered your Stripe credentials, let's customize the settings, as shown in the image below.

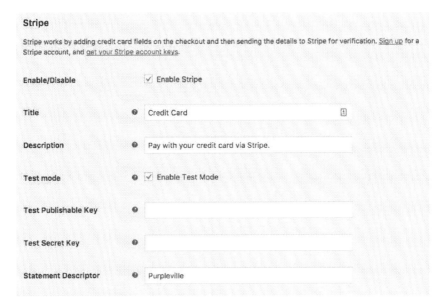

Stripe

Stripe works by adding credit card fields on the checkout and then sending the details to Stripe for verification. Sign up for a Stripe account, and get your Stripe account keys.

Enable/Disable	☑ Enable Stripe
Title ❓	Credit Card
Description ❓	Pay with your credit card via Stripe.
Test mode ❓	☑ Enable Test Mode
Test Publishable Key ❓	
Test Secret Key ❓	
Statement Descriptor ❓	Purpleville

- **Enable/Disable:** Check "Enable Stripe".
- **Title:** Credit Card
- **Description:** Pay with your credit card via Stripe.
- **Test mode:** Check "Enable Test Mode". Note: Be sure to turn off "Test Mode" when you launch your store.
- **Statement Descriptor:** Purpleville

The Statement Descriptor is what will show up on the customer's credit card statement, so try to be as clear as possible here. If you use something that people don't recognize, you'll get chargebacks just for displaying an unusual name and you'll lose valid payments.

What about the *Test Publishable Key* and *Test Secret Key* fields? For these, you'll need to head on over to http://stripe.com and create an account or log into your existing account.

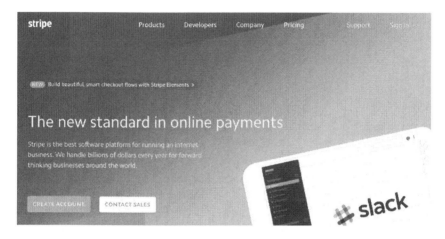

Once you've logged in, you'll be brought to a dashboard. This will show you all of your payments and details about each one. Very likely it will be empty at this point.

- Click on "API" in the left sidebar.

- You'll see a page where you can create keys. I already have my keys created, so I can just copy them. If you've never created API keys, you can create them at this point.

- But before you do – make sure you're viewing test data.
- Enable "Viewing test data".

- Copy the "Publishable key".
- Paste the key into the "Test Publishable Key" field in WooCommerce.

- Copy the "Secret key".
- Paste the key into the "Test Secret Key" field in WooCommerce.

Stripe

Stripe works by adding credit card fields on the checkout and then sending the details to Stripe for verification. Sign up for a Stripe account, and get your Stripe account keys.

Enable/Disable	✓ Enable Stripe
Title	Credit Card
Description	Pay with your credit card via Stripe.
Test mode	✓ Enable Test Mode
Test Publishable Key	pk_dljZMSfD4hLcNkk
Test Secret Key	
Statement Descriptor	Purpleville

- Hit "Save changes" at the bottom of the page.

Your site is now ready to accept credit cards.

When you're ready to go live, you can repeat these steps and disable *Test mode* in WooCommerce and copy over your live Stripe keys.

SETTING UP PAYPAL

Before we test our Stripe keys, let's configure our PayPal settings.

- Go to "WooCommerce" and then "Settings".
- Click on the "Checkout" tab.
- Click "Paypal" in the top menu, as shown below.

Now you can start to set up your site's PayPal integration:

- Check "Enable Paypal standard".
- **Title:** PayPal
- **Description:** Pay with PayPal; you can pay with with your credit card if you'd like.
- **PayPal Email:** Enter your PayPal email. The PayPal email is the address of the PayPal account to which the money will go.

PayPal

PayPal Standard sends customers to PayPal to enter their payment information. PayPal IPN requires fsockopen/cURL

Enable/Disable	☑ Enable PayPal Standard
Title	❷ PayPal
Description	❷ Pay via PayPal; you can pay with your credit card if you do
PayPal email	❷ payments@ostraining.com

- Click "Save changes" at the bottom of the page.

A quick note for later in the chpater: if you receive payments correctly from PayPal but they aren't marked as complete, there's probably something going on with the PayPal IPN. The IPN is how they notify you about successful payments. If that's the case, you definitely want to fill out the PayPal Identity Token. It allows for payments to be verified without the IPN. PayPal IPN works fine most of the time, but there are some hosts and configurations that just don't work that well. You can read more about how to set up the PayPal Identity Token here: https://docs.woocommerce.com/document/paypal-standard.

IPN Email Notifications	☑ Enable IPN email notifications
	Send notifications when an IPN is received from PayPal indicating refunds, chargebacks and cancellations.
Receiver email	❷ you@youremail.com
PayPal identity token	❷

TESTING THE CHECKOUT

Now it's time to test our checkout with the payment gateways enabled. Let's go to the product we created earlier and see what a customer would see.

- Visit your WooCommerce store, and you should see an image like the one below.

- Click "Add to cart" to add the product to our cart.

- You will then see a screen like the one below. That tells you that your product has been added to your cart. There's also a link to "View cart".

- Click "View cart" and you should see a screen similar to the one below.

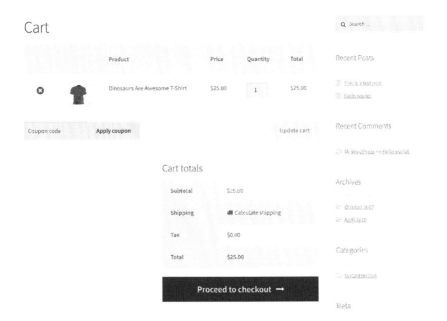

- We can click the black "Proceed to checkout" button.

Cart totals

Subtotal	$25.00
Shipping	Priority Mail: $6.65
	🚚 Calculate shipping
Tax	$0.92
Total	$32.57

Proceed to checkout →

- You will now see the "Billing details" stage of the checkout. Here customers can enter all of their billing information, plus also review their order and payment information.

- You might notice that some user information is filled out. If you're logged in (as a customer or admin), WooCommerce will prefill the fields with your user information.

- Fill out all of the information.

- Select "Credit Card" and fill out the test information.

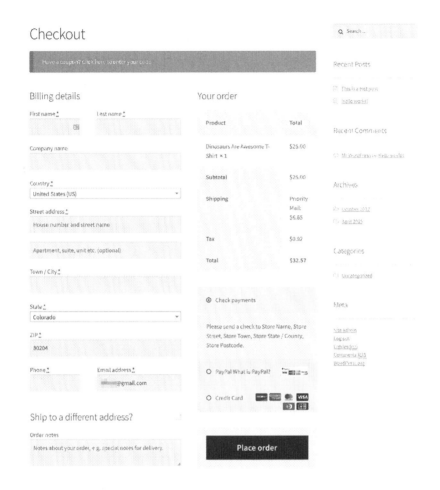

Checkout

Billing details

First name *   Last name *

Company name

Country *
United States (US)

Street address *
House number and street name

Apartment, suite, unit etc. (optional)

Town / City *

State *
Colorado

ZIP *
80204

Phone *   Email address *
@gmail.com

Ship to a different address?

Order notes
Notes about your order, e.g. special notes for delivery.

Your order

Product	Total
Dinosaurs Are Awesome T-Shirt × 1	$25.00
Subtotal	$25.00
Shipping	Priority Mail: $6.65
Tax	$0.92
Total	$32.57

Check payments

Please send a check to Store Name, Store Street, Store Town, Store State / County, Store Postcode.

PayPal What is PayPal?

Credit Card

Place order

Recent Posts

This is a test post
Hello world!

Recent Comments

Mr WordPress on Hello world!

Archives

October 2017
April 2015

Categories

Uncategorized

Meta

Site admin
Log out
Entries RSS
Comments RSS
WordPress.org

One little design feature I love about WooCommerce is when you're in test mode, they'll print out the test instructions for you.

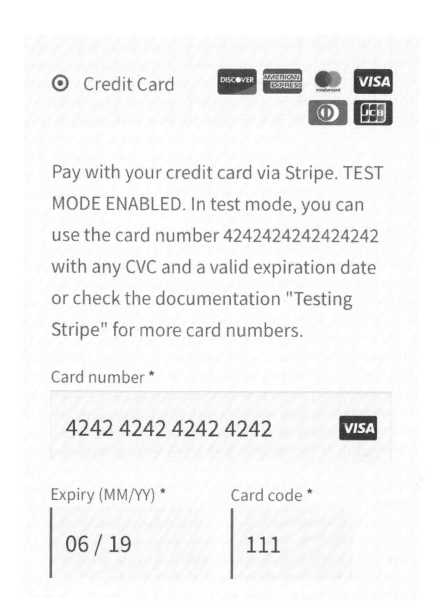

Credit Card

Pay with your credit card via Stripe. TEST MODE ENABLED. In test mode, you can use the card number 4242424242424242 with any CVC and a valid expiration date or check the documentation "Testing Stripe" for more card numbers.

Card number *

4242 4242 4242 4242   VISA

Expiry (MM/YY) *   Card code *

06 / 19   111

- Click "Place order".
- You should then see the "Order received" page, like the image below.

This page reiterates all the details of our purchase, as well as shipping details and contact details. The customer could print this, but they will also get an email of this information.

Huzzah! We completed an order and did everything except use real money. We know that we just need to run on Live mode instead of Test mode.

- If we open up "Orders" under the WooCommerce side menu, we can see the order that we just placed.

WHAT'S NEXT?

At this point, your Checkout process is working! If you wanted to you could turn on live mode, accept real payments, and start fulfilling this order.

However, before we launch our store, let's look at a few more types of products that you may want to sell.

Turn the page to find out more about selling digital products in your WooCommerce store.

CHAPTER 6.

WOOCOMMERCE DIGITAL PRODUCTS EXPLAINED

In this chapter, we are going to look at how to set up a digital product with WooCommerce.

A digital product consists of downloadable files that will be automatically emailed to the customer after payment.

Since we love all things purple here in Purpleville, we decided to design a desktop background for our own computer. And hey, it's a digital product. We might as well sell it, right?

ADDING A DIGITAL PRODUCT

- In the admin area of your WordPress site, go to "Products" and then "Add New".
- Add a new product called "Stylish Abstract Purple Desktop Wallpaper".
- Add a description.

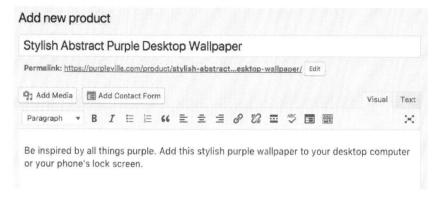

Add new product

Stylish Abstract Purple Desktop Wallpaper

Permalink: https://purpleville.com/product/stylish-abstract...esktop-wallpaper/ Edit

Add Media   Add Contact Form   Visual Text

Paragraph ▼ B I ≣ ≣ 66 ≣ ≣ ≣ 𝒫 ⅔ ⊞ ᴬᴮᶜ⌄ ⊞ ⊞   ⨯

Be inspired by all things purple. Add this stylish purple wallpaper to your desktop computer or your phone's lock screen.

- Type in a new category called "Wallpapers".
- Click "Add new category" and "Wallpapers" should be automatically selected.

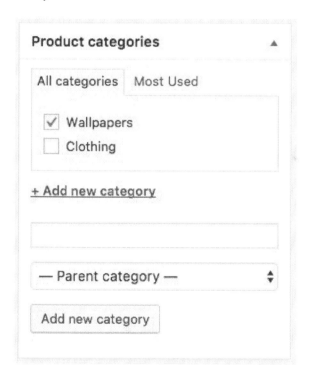

Product categories ▲

All categories | Most Used

☑ Wallpapers
☐ Clothing

+ Add new category

— Parent category — ⬍

Add new category

- Scroll down to the section titled "Product Data".
- Select both the "Virtual" and "Downloadable" boxes.

Product data —	Simple product	⇕	Virtual: ☑	Downloadable: ☑
🖋 General	Regular price (£)			
◈ Inventory	Sale price (£)			_Schedule_

It's important to note that most but not all virtual products are downloadable. Virtual means there is no physical product. Downloadable means there's a file that's downloaded. So if you sell a membership (to your site, or perhaps to a service), that would be a virtual but *not* downloadable product.

Also, if you sold a video game that includes a downloadable file and a backup CD, that would be a downloadable file but *not* virtual. This is because there is a physical component that needs to be shipped.

In our example we have a downloadable file and no physical product, so we select both "Virtual" and "Downloadable".

You may notice that the "Shipping" tab disappeared. This is because virtual products don't need any shipping data. Instead of "Shipping," a new "Downloadable files" area has appeared.

- **Regular Price ($):** $10

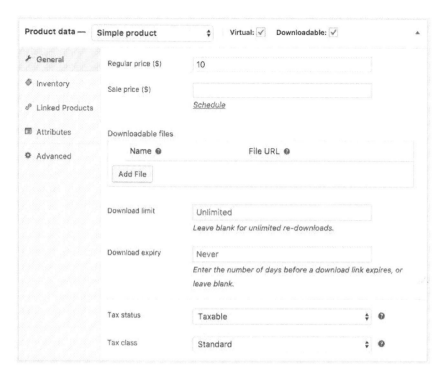

- Locate the section called "Downloadable files".

- Click on "Add File". Upload the file called stylish-abstract-purple-background.jpg from your Resources folder.

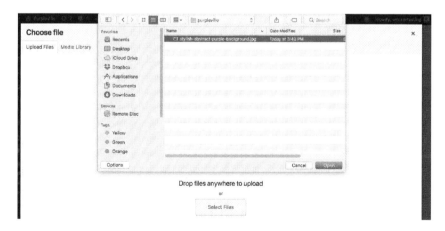

- Click the "Insert file URL" button in the bottom right corner.

You'll now see a "File URL" filled out and an optional "File name" field, as shown below.

- Leave the "File name" blank and allow it to use the file name that is in the URL.

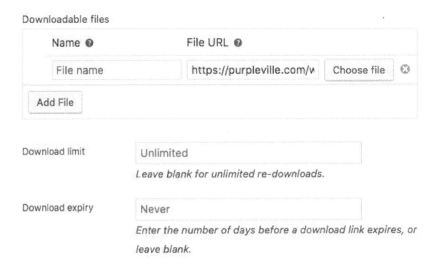

You'll see there are two fields: "Download limit" and "Download expiry":

- **Download Limit:** This determines how many times the person who purchased the product may download it. I honestly don't recommend setting a limit. The point is to prevent piracy, but any good pirate will download it once and be able to distribute it however they want. But if a user ever does start sharing a download link, you could shut it down by setting a limit such as 5 or 10.

- **Download Expiry:** This determines the days before the download expires from the time the customer purchased it. Again the point is to prevent piracy, and a good pirate can get around this. So I'll leave mine blank.

Download limit	Unlimited
	Leave blank for unlimited re-downloads.
Download expiry	Never
	Enter the number of days before a download link expires, or leave blank.

Let's keep moving on with the settings:

- Leave "Download Limit" to "Unlimited".

- Leave "Download Expiry" to "Never".

- Leave the "Short Description" blank for now.

- However, we will add a "Product Image" for this product. Choose the same stylish-abstract-purple-background.jpg file that you uploaded earlier in the chapter.

- Click "Publish" and take a look at our newly created product.

Your screen should look similar to the one below.

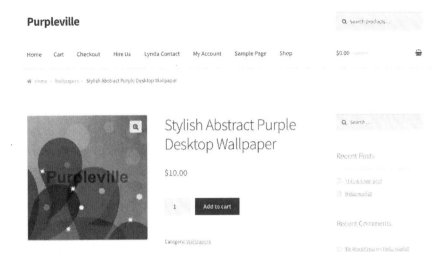

TESTING YOUR DIGITABLE PRODUCT

Now, let's test it out the second product in our WooCommerce store.

- Click on "Add to cart" and then "View cart".
- Click "Proceed to checkout" and you should see a screen similar to the one below.
- All my information is already loaded in here from before, so let's click on "Credit Card".

Checkout

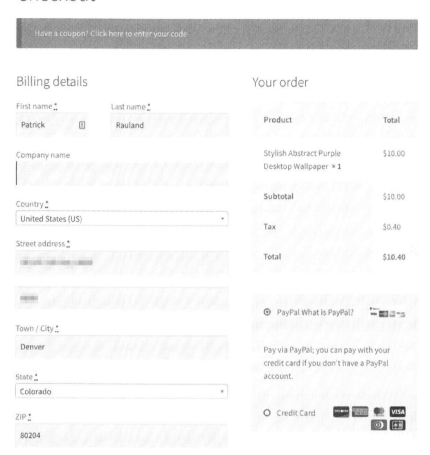

Have a coupon? Click here to enter your code

Billing details

First name *
Patrick

Last name *
Rauland

Company name

Country *
United States (US)

Street address *

Town / City *
Denver

State *
Colorado

ZIP *
80204

Your order

Product	Total
Stylish Abstract Purple Desktop Wallpaper × 1	$10.00
Subtotal	$10.00
Tax	$0.40
Total	$10.40

⊙ PayPal What is PayPal?

Pay via PayPal; you can pay with your credit card if you don't have a PayPal account.

○ Credit Card

- We still have Test Mode active from the previous time. Enter a test credit card number.

- Then click "Place Order" and you should see a screen like the one below.

Order received

Thank you. Your order has been received.

ORDER NUMBER:
55

DATE:
December 13, 2017

EMAIL:

TOTAL:
$10.40

PAYMENT METHOD:
Credit Card

**You can download the file(s) here
or via a link in your email**

Downloads

Product	Downloads remaining	Expires	Download
Stylish Abstract Purple Desktop Wallpaper	∞	Never	stylish-abstract-purple-background.jpg

- You can see all of the details about your order on this screen.
- You can click the file name under "Downloads" and you'll immediately download the file. Or, you can check your email for the email receipt and download the file there.

DIGITAL PRODUCT ORDERS IN WOOCOMMERCE

Now let's check what that digital product orders look like in WooCommerce.

- Go to your admin area, then "WooCommerce" and then "Orders". You will see a screen like the one below.

Notice the blue check mark next to order #55? That means the order is complete. There's nothing we have to do.

The green "…" next to order #36 means the order is processing. In WooCommerce, "processing" means we've received payment and we need to ship products. So with our previous order, WooCommerce is telling us that we still need to ship the product. However, with digital products, once we receive payment, WooCommerce automatically fires off an email and we're done. Awesome, right?

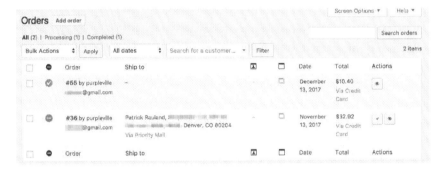

DIGITAL PRODUCT ORDERS ON THE FRONT-END

Let's check that the digital product order is marked as complete on the front-end of our site.

On the "My Account" page, we can see all of our purchases. And we can click on "View" to see specific order details. We can also click on the "Downloads" tab to see all of our available downloads.

Orders

		Order	Date	Status	Total	Actions
Dashboard						
Orders		#55	December 13, 2017	Completed	$10.40 for 1 item	View
Downloads		#36	November 13, 2017	Processing	$32.92 for 1 item	View
Addresses						
Payment methods						
Account details						
Logout						

WHAT'S NEXT?

We've set up simple products and we can now offer digital files with our products. Next, we will cover variable products.

Variable products are more complicated, but they're the most flexible type of product. They let the user choose from a few different options for each product. You, as the store owner, have the power to choose different images, different stock, and even different pricing for each variation.

CHAPTER 7.

WOOCOMMERCE ATTRIBUTES AND VARIATIONS EXPLAINED

In this chapter, we are going to take a look at product attributes and variations.

Attributes are useful when searching for and filtering products. There are some WooCommerce widgets that help users filter products. If you give attributes to products, users can filter using them.

Variations are useful because they allow users to choose different options on the product page. This means you can sell a T-Shirt in different sizes and colors. You can do this using one product with a few different variations.

As we'll see, there's a good reason why we've included both attributes and variations in the same chapter. They often rely on each other to work effectively. We're going to start by creating attributes, because that's an essential first step before creating variations.

SETTING UP ATTRIBUTES

Earlier in the book we created our purple dinosaur shirt, which only has one style. Now, we're going to sell a new shirt that comes in different styles. There will be a polo shirt, a t-shirt with a regular circle neck, and a t-shirt with a u-neck. We want our users to pick the style that works for them. We can do this by setting up attributes. Then we can create variations using those attributes.

- Go to "Products" and then "Attributes" from your left sidebar menu.

- By default, no attributes are set up in a WooCommerce store.

- We are going to create a name for our first attribute. We could call it "neck lines" to be very specific, but let's just call them "Styles" since our users will have an easier time understanding that.

- Name the new attribute "Styles".

- The slug will automatically be created, and we can leave the rest of these options untouched. They primarily control how you can search for attributes.

- Click "Add attribute" and your attribute will be added.

Attributes

Add new attribute

Attributes let you define extra product data, such as size or color. You can use these attributes in the shop sidebar using the "layered nav" widgets. Please note: you cannot rename an attribute later on.

Name

Styles

Name for the attribute (shown on the front-end).

Slug

Unique slug/reference for the attribute; must be no more than 28 characters.

☐ Enable Archives?

Enable this if you want this attribute to have product archives in your store.

Type

Select ‡

*Determines how you select attributes for products. Under admin panel -> products -> product data -> attributes -> values, **Text** allows manual entry whereas **select** allows pre-configured terms in a drop-down list.*

Default sort order

Custom ordering ‡

Determines the sort order of the terms on the frontend shop product pages. If using custom ordering, you can drag and drop the terms in this attribute.

Add attribute

CONFIGURING THE TERMS

Now that we have created our attribute, we can create some different styles.

- Click "Configure terms" in the same row as "Styles".

Let's add our three types of styles: Polo, Circle Neck, and U Neck. You'll have to do them one at a time.

- Enter the Product Style Name.
- Give it a short description.
- Click "Add new style".

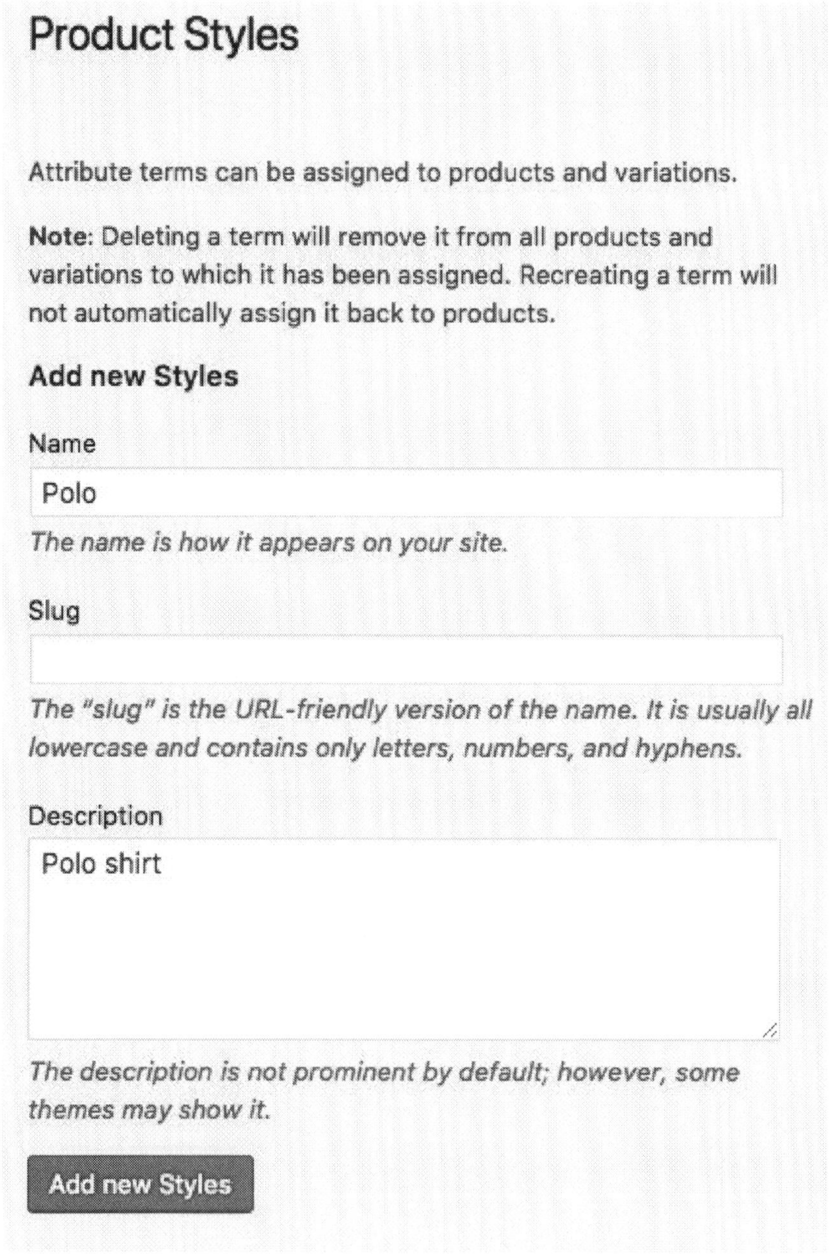

Product Styles

Attribute terms can be assigned to products and variations.

Note: Deleting a term will remove it from all products and variations to which it has been assigned. Recreating a term will not automatically assign it back to products.

Add new Styles

Name

Polo

The name is how it appears on your site.

Slug

The "slug" is the URL-friendly version of the name. It is usually all lowercase and contains only letters, numbers, and hyphens.

Description

Polo shirt

The description is not prominent by default; however, some themes may show it.

Add new Styles

- You'll know you're done when you see the completed list, as in the image below.

- To see the terms, go to "Products" and then "Attributes".

This was a lot of work! It took numerous screens to get our styles set up. But what we've done will make it much easier to create variable products. We'll choose our options from a drop down instead of having to type everything out manually.

SETTING UP A VARIABLE PRODUCT

Let's start by creating a new product.

- In your WordPress admin, hover over "Products" and click "New Product".

- Enter "Plain Purple Shirt" as the title for this product.

- From the "Product Type" drop down, choose "Variable product".

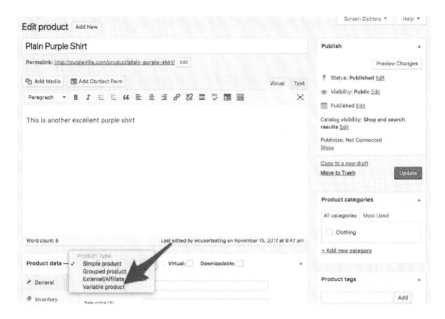

And let's add our attributes.

- From the Product data meta box, click "Attributes".

- Select "Styles" followed by "Add".

- Select "Used for variations" and "Select all".

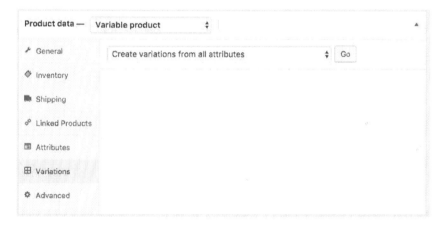

- Click "Save attributes".

- Click on the "Variations" tab.

- And from the drop down, select "Create variations from all attributes" followed by "Go".

- You'll see an alert pop up. Click "OK".

You should now see your three variations, as shown in the screen below.

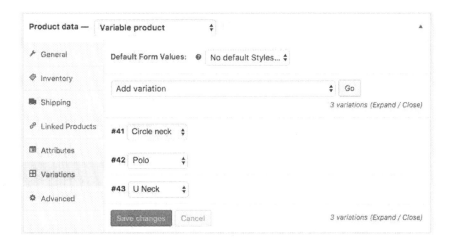

You can click into each one and change specific things.

You can enter a price specific to this variation. You can choose a custom weight and dimensions – in the case of shirts, perhaps some sizes are physically larger than others. You can specify which variations are in stock.

In this example, let's upload a custom photo for this variation. That will help the user make the right choice.

- Click the "Photo" icon and upload the file called shirt-circle.jpg from your Resources folder.

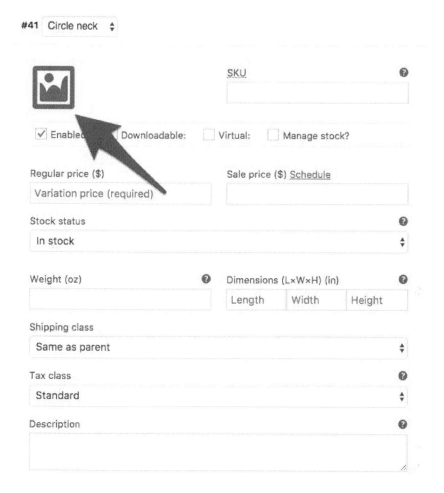

- Repeat this for the U Neck and Polo variations. The files called shirt-uneck.jpg and shirt-polo.jpg are in your Resources folder.

- When you're done, don't forget to click "Save changes".

- And then just for good measure, click "Update" (or "Publish" if the product wasn't already published) just to make sure all of the data is saved.

Let's take a look at this product on the front-end.

When the user chooses a style, they'll see updated pricing and an updated photo. If you see a message about the product being unavailable, you probably forgot to set a price for each variation.

Using variable products makes your store much easier to navigate for the end user. And you have less information to manage.

Setting up those attributes is a pain to do the first time. But once they're set up, creating variable products isn't too hard.

Attributes also display on the front end and make your product page a little easier to read for humans and search bots.

Description

Additional information

Additional information   >   Styles   Circle neck, Polo, U Neck

Reviews (0)

If you ever want to add custom information to the "Additional information" tab, you can manually type in attributes on the edit product page.

An example of another store doing this is Best Buy. If we look at one of their products, we can see a large amount of attributes. How far you want to go with attributes is entirely up to you. The more information that you provide for your customers, the more likely they are to buy because they feel safe and secure knowing everything about the product. So I recommend putting in as many attributes as you can.

WHAT'S NEXT?

Congrats on setting up a variable product! This is arguably the hardest thing with WooCommerce. There's a lot to think about with attributes and variations. If you can build your product pages with variable products, the rest of WooCommerce should be pretty easy to set up.

Now it's time to start customizing the front end of the store. We'll customize what we show users and how we organize our products.

CHAPTER 8.

WOOCOMMERCE LAYOUTS AND WIDGETS EXPLAINED

In this chapter, we're going to take a look at layout options for our WooCommerce store.

The example we're going to use is setting up our site's homepage.

By default WordPress will show a list of posts on the homepage. Because we're running an e-commerce site, we need our homepage to show our products.

SETTING YOUR SHOP PAGE AS YOUR HOMEPAGE

In order to change our site's homepage, we need to make a change in the WordPress admin area.

- Go to "Settings" and then "Reading".
- Make sure that "A static page" is chosen.
- Change the "Homepage" option to "Shop".

If you make this change, you will have lost the blog post on the frontpage. If you still want to write blog posts, here's what to do:

- Go to "Pages".
- Create a new page called "News".
- Go back to "Settings" and then "Reading".
- Set the "Posts page" option to your new page.

Now when you reload the homepage, you see the shop page. In the image below, you can see three products on my "Shop" page.

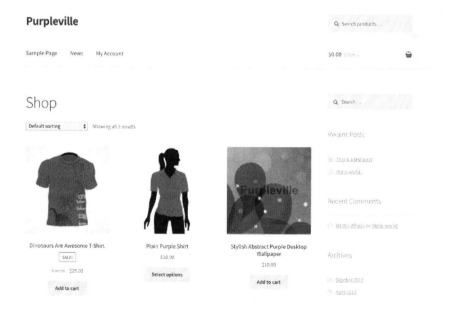

EDITING YOUR SHOP PAGE

We can change the way this "Shop" page looks. For one thing, I would like to say something at the top. Fortunately this is just a regular page in WordPress, so we can edit it.

- In the WordPress admin, go to "Pages" and edit the "Shop" page.
- Add some welcome text to your homepage.

When we reload the homepage, we can see the text displayed at the top. This means that you can really put anything you want in here, such as images, a slideshow or anything else you wish.

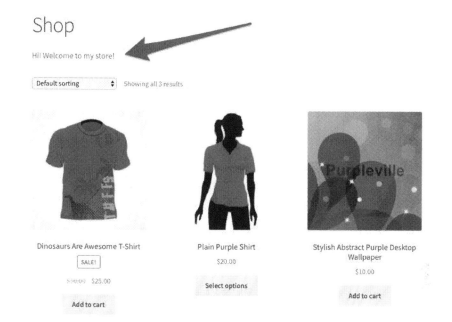

CHANGING YOUR SHOP DISPLAY

- Go to "Appearance" and then "Customize".
- From here you'll want to select "WooCommerce".

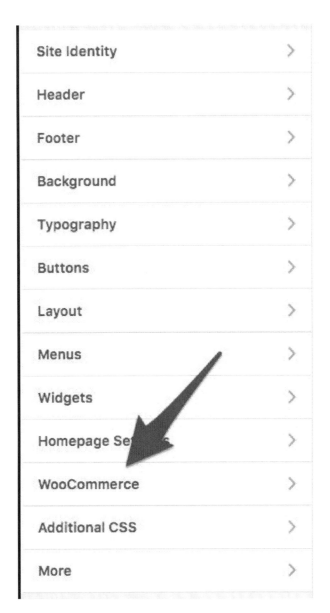

Site Identity	>
Header	>
Footer	>
Background	>
Typography	>
Buttons	>
Layout	>
Menus	>
Widgets	>
Homepage Se s	>
WooCommerce	>
Additional CSS	>
More	>

- Click on the "Product Catalog".

As you can see in the image below, the "Shop page display" is currently set to "Show Products".

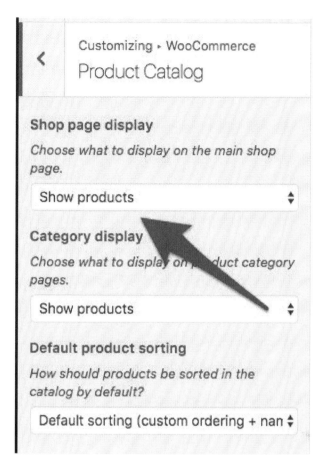

Customizing ▸ WooCommerce

Product Catalog

Shop page display

Choose what to display on the main shop page.

Show products ⬍

Category display

Choose what to display on product category pages.

Show products ⬍

Default product sorting

How should products be sorted in the catalog by default?

Default sorting (custom ordering + nan ⬍

- Alternatively, we can set "Shop page display" to "Show categories" or "Show categories & products".

- Choose "Show categories". You should instantly see categories instead of products.
- Click "Publish" at the top of the Customizer tab to save your changes.

Shop

Hi! Welcome to my store!

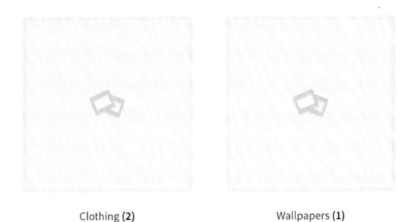

Clothing (2)   Wallpapers (1)

ADDING IMAGES TO YOUR CATEGORIES

This new version of the "Shop" page looks boring, so let's include some images here.

- Go to "Products" and then "Categories".
- We can see all of our categories from this view, as shown in the image below.

Let's add an image to the "Clothing" category.

- Click "Clothing" and you should see an "Edit category" screen like the one below.
- You'll see we can "Upload/Add image" for the category here.
- Upload the clothes-category.png image from your Resources folder.

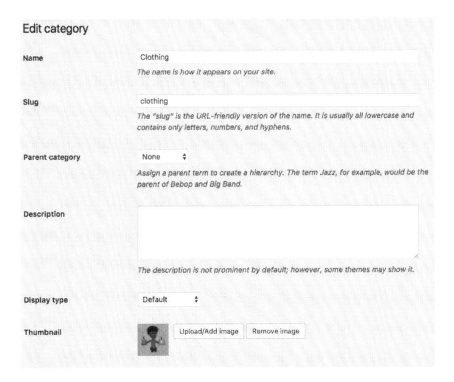

- Repeat this process to edit the Wallpapers category. You can use the wallpaper image that you uploaded earlier in the book.

- Now when you reload your homepage, each category has its own image, as you see in the image below.

Shop

Hi! Welcome to my store!

Clothing **(2)**

Wallpapers **(1)**

DISPLAYING BOTH PRODUCTS AND CATEGORIES

We have another option that builds on what we've seen so far: we could choose to show both products and categories.

- Go to "Appearance" and then "Customize".
- Click on "WooCommerce" and then "Product Catalog".
- For the "Shop page display" click on "Show categories & products".
- Reload your homepage, and your screen should look similar to the one below.

I don't love this setting. I find that it can be confusing for the user. I assume there are different products in the categories and these products are uncategorized (which isn't the case). So be careful with this setting. I recommend either showing products or categories, but not both on the same screen.

Clothing **(2)**   Wallpapers **(1)**   Dinosaurs Are Awesome T-Shirt

SALE!

~~$30.00~~ $25.00

Add to cart

Plain Purple Shirt   Stylish Abstract Purple Desktop
$20.00   Wallpaper

                                 $10.00

Select options   Add to cart

ADDING CHILD CATEGORIES

We can also add child categories, or in other words, subcategories.

Let's make "Clothing" a parent category for "T-Shirts".

- Go to "Products" and then "Categories".
- Let's type the name of our category into "Name".
- Select the "Clothing" category as the "Parent category".

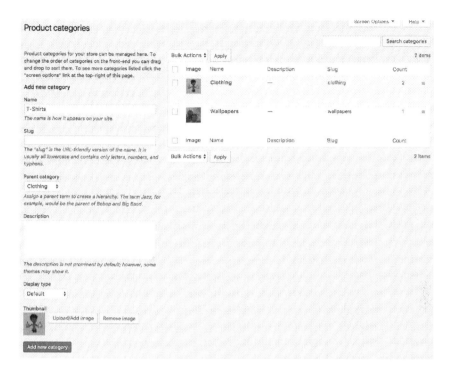

Product categories

Let's change our products to be in the t-shirt category instead of the clothing category. Now is a good time to show off the Bulk Edit feature.

- Go to "Products".

- Check the checkmark next to all of the products you want to edit.

- Then select "Edit" from the "Bulk Actions" dropdown.

- Then click "Apply".

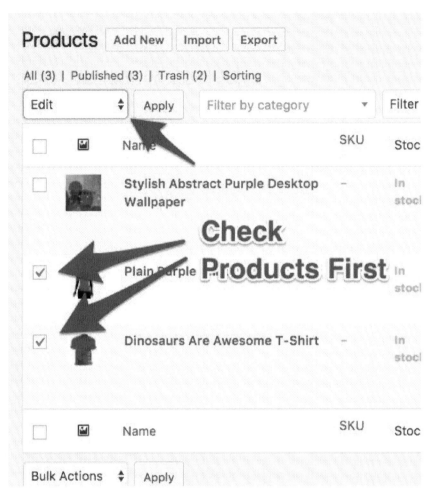

- A new editable menu will appear, which you can see below.
- Check the correct category.
- Then click "Update".

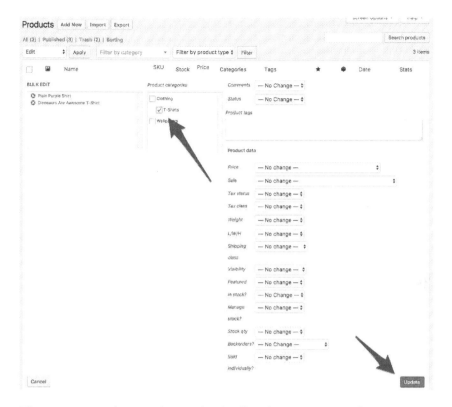

There is one downside to the bulk editor. You can't remove a category this way. You have to go into each product and manually deselect the previous category.

- Click a product title to edit it.
- Deselect a category.
- Click "Update".

Repeat the above steps for all of your products.

If we want to display the child category, or subcategory, we can do so by changing some settings.

- Go to "Appearance" and then "Customize".
- Click on the "WooCommerce" and then "Product Catalog".

- Under "Category display" you can select a few different options.

Notice that the Category Display is set to "Show products". However, we want it to display subcategories.

- For "Category Display" select "Show subcategories".

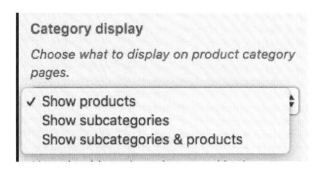

- Click "Publish" to save your changes.

To test this we can either stay in the customizer or go to the front end of our site and click into our "Clothing" category page. After doing this, we will see our subcategory "T-Shirts".

Clothing

T-Shirts **(2)**

Again, I don't recommend showing both categories and products on the same page. If you have a lot of products, then I suggest only showing categories and creating a good hierarchy of parent and child categories so that people can narrow down their search criteria.

If you only have a few products, or not many in your categories, then I would suggest not listing the categories at all and just showing products.

I'm going to go back to my display settings and only show categories.

ADDING CATEGORIES TO THE SIDEBAR WIDGET

At the moment, our sidebar category widget doesn't actually list our product categories, as you can see below. Let's go ahead and change that.

- Go to "Appearance" and then "Widgets".
- You'll probably see a widget area called "Sidebar" filled with default widgets:

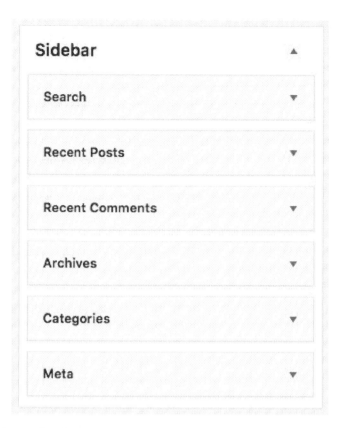

- Click on the down arrow icon.
- Then click "Delete".
- Repeat the above steps to clear out the existing widget area.

- In the list of available widgets, click "Product Search".
- Make sure "Sidebar" is selected and click "Add Widget".

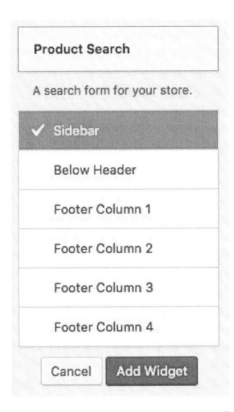

- Repeat the above with the "Product categories" widget
- Now you can see all our product categories in our sidebar and product search, as shown below. It even shows category hierarchy.

Q Search products...

Product categories

▢ Clothing

▢ T-Shirts

▢ Wallpapers

How you organize the layout of your store is entirely up to you, there isn't a right or wrong way to do it.

You may want to test different layouts to see how your customers respond. Try two different layouts for a while and see which one gets you more sales. Testing can be an extremely valuable part of your e-commerce store, and I highly recommend that you run as many tests as you can to see what kind of changes get more sales.

EXPLORING WIDGETS

Now that we've seen what the "WooCommerce Products Category" widget does, let's explore other WooCommerce widgets. WooCommerce actually comes with quite a few different widgets.

• Go to "Appearance" -> "Customize" -> "Widgets".

• Open up the "Sidebar" area.

One of the most important widgets if you're not using the

Storefront theme is "WooCommerce Cart," which displays the user's cart in the sidebar. We already have that built into the header of our theme so we can skip it. But if you don't have a theme with a cart widget built in, you'll want to add this one.

If we have a look at some of the other widgets available, we will see that there are three widgets that help us filter products. You can select to "Filter Products by Attribute," "Filter Products by Rating," and "Filter Products by Price". You can see the descriptions of each in the image below.

	Filter Products by Attribute
	Display a list of attributes to filter products in your store.
Filter Products by Price	Filter Products by Rating
Display a slider to filter products in your store by price.	Display a list of star ratings to filter products in your store.

All of these are useful. If you have attributes like different colors, sizes, or cuts, that's a really helpful way to organize your store. Filtering by price is another good option. Price is easier to set up and is helpful on just about any store. Let's set that one up.

- Add the "Filter Products by Price" widget to our "Sidebar".

- If you go to a page that shows products, you'll see the widget appear.

There are a few more widgets that we can add including "Recently Viewed," "Recently Reviewed," and "Product Tag Cloud".

"Recent Reviews" simply lists the most recent reviews on the site. Since we don't have any at the moment, that would be blank. So, let's skip this one for now.

- Let's add "Recently Viewed Products".

- Now let's save and publish.

You will note that our "Recently Viewed" widget isn't currently displaying a product. The reason for this is because it hasn't started keeping track.

- So, let's view a product now.

- Now that we've viewed a product, you should see that it is now displayed in our sidebar under our "Recently Viewed Products" widget.

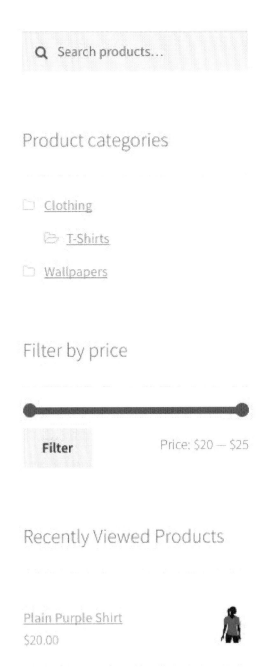

So as you can see, you can stock up your sidebar with some great features that help make your store more pleasant and easier to use.

WHAT'S NEXT?

We started with the default product layout. Now we have categories and featured images for those categories. We also added widgets that help the user browse our catalog.

Next, we'll look into how you can customize the look and feel of your theme.

CHAPTER 9.

WOOCOMMERCE THEMES EXPLAINED

One of the best things about WordPress is that the functionality and design of your site are totally separate. You can change your site's theme and people will still be able to browse, add products to the cart, and checkout.

That sounds obvious, but plenty of other eCommerce platforms don't work this way. In many other platforms, if you change the way a product page looks, it might break that product page.

In this chapter, we are going to take a look at a variety of themes. We'll also look at different ways you can customize those themes.

EXPLORING THE STOREFRONT THEME

The theme we've been using thus far is Storefront.

We took a tour of a Storefront site in the chapter called "Touring a WooCommerce Site Explained". You can find our more information about Storefront from inside your WordPress site.

- Go to "Appearance" then "Storefront".

You'll now see the screen shown below. On this page they recommend enhancements to Storefront. The WooCommerece team also recommend a bundle and promote some industry-specific child themes. Since the child themes are hard to modify, we'll just stay with the main Storefront theme and customize that.

The other link I want to point out is the "Development blog". This is hosted at https://woocommerce.wordpress.com and is where the WooCommerce developers talk about everything new that goes into Storefront. If you are a developer, I recommend subscribing to the blog for email updates. There's only a few updates per year so it should be pretty easy to follow.

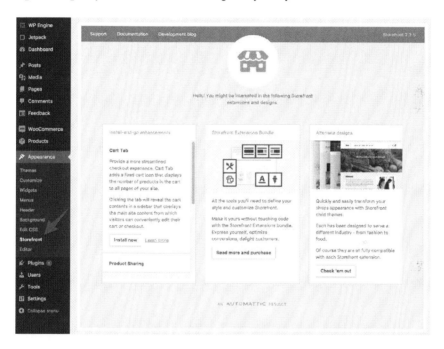

CUSTOMIZING THE STOREFRONT THEME

Let's customize the Storefront theme for the first time.

- Go to "Appearance" then "Customize".

- This will open the WordPress customizer. This gives us a visual representation of our theme. There is a menu on the left side that let's us customize the different site elements.

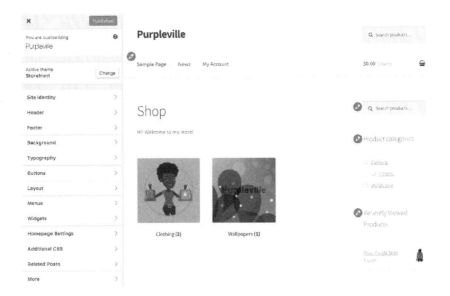

- Click "Site Identity" which is the top menu link in the left sidebar.

This will show us a few different important options, like the name of our site. We have the name already (Purpleville) but we don't have a tagline or icon. Let's add both of those.

- Type in your tagline.
- Upload an image for your icon. It should be square and at least 512px by 512px.

I've gone ahead and reused our desktop background from earlier since it's purple and matches our brand. You can see a preview of what the icon looks like in Chrome in the screenshot below.

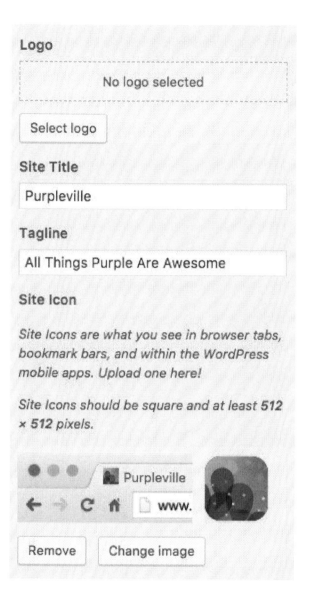

Logo

No logo selected

Select logo

Site Title

Purpleville

Tagline

All Things Purple Are Awesome

Site Icon

Site Icons are what you see in browser tabs, bookmark bars, and within the WordPress mobile apps. Upload one here!

Site Icons should be square and at least 512 × 512 pixels.

Purpleville

www.

Remove   Change image

There is one important thing to note about the Customizer: nothing is saved until you click "Publish". As you make changes, they will only be visible to you. To actually see any of these changes live on your site, remember to click "Publish".

Let's keep customizing our theme since there's so much more we can do.

- Click on the back arrow to go back to all customizer options.
- Click "Header" so we can edit those settings.

On this page we can add an image background for the header. We can also choose a font color for the text in the header. That's mostly our site name, tagline, and links.

My recommendation is to go with either a light background and dark text or a dark background and light text. You want to make sure everything is crystal clear. In the example below, I'm using a solid purple color.

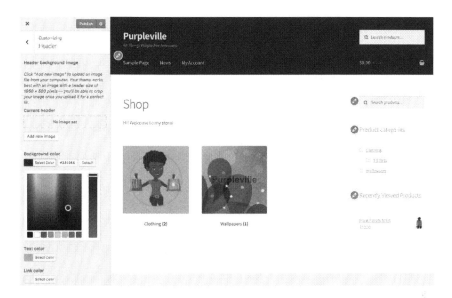

- Set "Background color" to #330066
- Set "Text color" to #AAAAAA
- Set "Link color" to #EEEEEE

This looks much better.

- Click the back arrow to go back to all Customizer settings.

Now let's customize the footer.

- Click "Footer" to open the footer settings.

Here we see options to customize the background and some font colors. We're going to repeat a lot of what we did earlier.

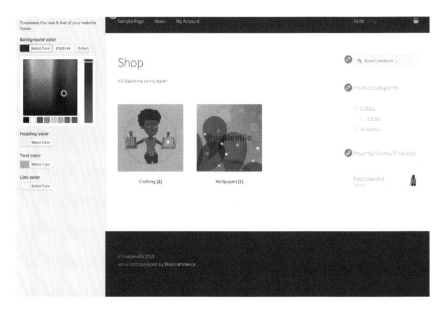

- Set "Background color" to #330066
- Set "Heading color" to #EEEEEE
- Set "Text color" to #AAAAAA
- Set "Link color" to #EEEEEE

Now our footer matches our header.

Now I want to customize our product page. We can change a few things with the built in controls built into this theme. But with a plugin we can do even more. We're going to install a free plugin called WooCommerce Colors that lets us change some WooCommerce specific settings, like the add to cart button color.

Don't forget that we have to save all of the work we did!

- Click "Publish" in the top of the customizer.

Now we're ready to install that plugin:

- Click the "X" button to exit the customizer.

- Click "Plugins" from the admin menu.
- Click "Add New".
- Type in "WooCommerce Colors" and you should see it.

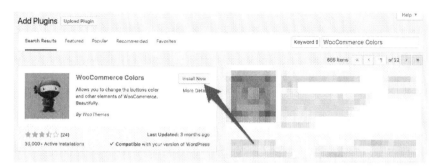

- Click "Install Now".
- Click "Activate".

The plugin is installed and ready to go. We can play with the settings within the customizer. So let's go back to that.

- Click "Appearance".
- Click "Customize".

Now we want to navigate directly to a product page. We can do this in the customizer. Click through your categories until you see a list of products.

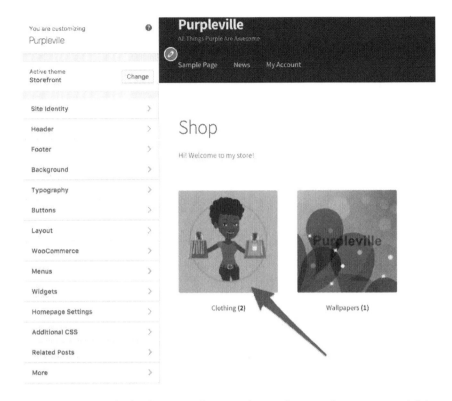

Now we can click that product and see the product page within the customizer.

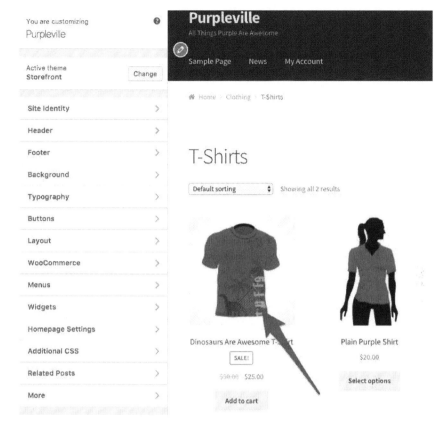

We're on the correct page. Now let's open the right menu.

- Click "WooCommerce" in the customizer menu.

Here we can see five options:

- Primary Color
- Secondary Color
- Highlight Color
- Content Background Color
- Subtext Color

Not all will apply to all themes, and the colors you see listed won't immediately appear on the product page. This is a minor issue with the plugin. But as soon as you start changing the colors, you will see them reflected on the product page.

- Set "Primary Color" to #8224E3, and you'll see the "Add to cart" button change.

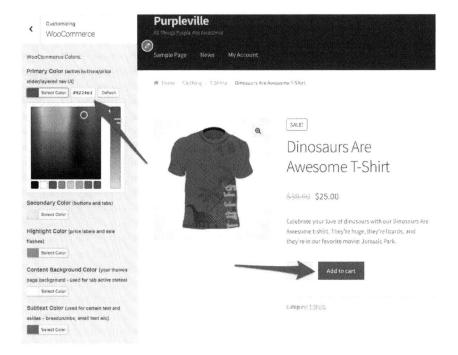

We don't need to change all of these colors. The only other one I recommend you play with is the "Highlight Color". This is used for the sale price, and you really want to highlight those sales badges and sale prices. Common convention is to use a reddish color. Since we're Purplesville, I'll make it a pink-red color.

- Set "Highlight Color" to #C9026F

The product page, home page, and the whole site looks a lot better. Let's not forget to save these changes.

- Click "Publish" at the top of the customizer.

You can now go to the front end of the website if you want to double check that everything looks correct.

There are plenty of other settings you can tweak in the Customizer. There are also plenty of other plugins that add even more customization options to your WooCommerce store. Before looking for a new theme I recommend playing with these settings to see if you can accomplish you goals with Storefront, since it is the go-to theme for WooCommerce.

TWENTY SEVENTEEN THEME

There are over 500 themes on WordPress.org that are tagged with WooCommerce. We'll look at one of the themes that comes with WordPress as another example of a good starter theme.

Let's take a look at a very basic theme. Twenty Seventeen is the latest official theme from the WordPress team.

- From the left menu, go to "Appearance" and then "Themes".
- Scroll until you find "Twenty Seventeen" or you can search for it.
- Click "Live Preview".

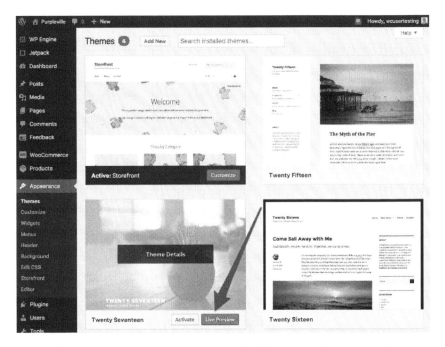

- You'll now see your store but in the "Twenty Seventeen" theme, as shown in the image below.

As you can see, this theme focuses on a giant image that takes up the entire screen until you scroll down. Once you scroll down, you'll see our list of products.

This theme not only has a giant header image on the home page – it also has a giant photo on each product page. This theme might work really well if you have a high quality product where people expect high quality images.

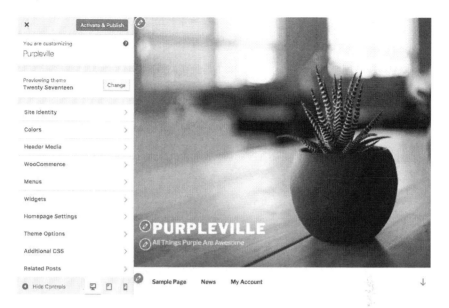

Let's see how a product page looks in this theme.

- Click on a category until you get to a product page.

Our single product page looks pretty nice. You can see that you need to have really good photography for this type of layout to work for you. And again that's the power of WordPress, you can pick a theme that works for your business.

However, we're not going to use the Twenty Seventeen theme live on your site, so do not click "Activate & Publish".

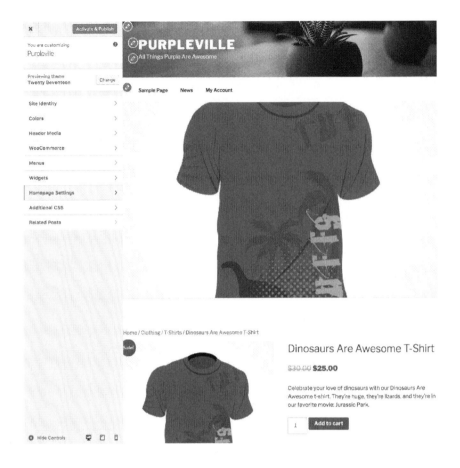

DECLARING WOOCOMMERCE SUPPORT

If you browse through the many hundreds of free themes on WordPress.org, or if you pay for a theme from a theme store, you might come across a banner that that's "Your theme does not declare WooCommerce support".

This doesn't necessarily mean anything. WooCommerce works so well with most themes that it most likely isn't an issue. But it does mean you should double check and make sure you can navigate through the product, cart, and checkout pages just to double check everything still works.

You can also ask the theme author if their theme supports WooCommerce.

BACK TO STOREFRONT

The best theme I've seen is Storefront. It's the official theme from WooCommerce. It's free and there are Storefront extensions to make it do anything we need.

WooCommerce should work with any theme but will probably need some minor tweaks. You will end up doing some things whether it be through adding plugins, changing settings or actually getting into some CSS and making it look different.

Since Storefront is best for Purpleville, and it's very likely best for your project, we're going to keep our theme set to Storefront.

WHAT'S NEXT?

We were finally able to customize the look and feel of our theme. It's often the first thing a new store owner wants to do – but I always recommend doing it after your store works the way you want. That way you can preview exactly what your customers will see when they navigate your store.

By now you should have all of your colors selected. You can always update your colors down the line if you need to – so go ahead and make some initial color changes just to experiment.

Next we'll look into some extensions for WooCommerce. These let you add advanced functionality to your store.

CHAPTER 10.

WOOCOMMERCE EXTENSIONS EXPLAINED

In this chapter, we are going to take a look at some of the extensions available for WooCommerce. In doing so, we'll specifically look at price to give you a better idea about how much it really costs to set up a WooCommerce store.

You can view these extensions at http://ostra.in/woo-ext. Let's explore some of our options available to use as WooCommerce users.

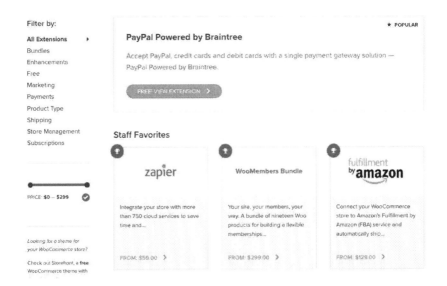

Two of the most useful categories are payment gateways and shipping methods.

Earlier in the book, we set up two payment gateways, Stripe and PayPal. We also set up the USPS for shipping, thanks to the WooCommerce onboarding wizard. If you're building this for yourself as a test, I strongly recommend you stick with these defaults. They're incredibly easy to use and cost you nothing. If you're launching a real site, you may need to choose different options, particularly if you're not in the USA.

PAYMENT GATEWAY EXTENSIONS

However, many times you may already have a preferred payment gateway like Authorize.Net, First Data, Amazon Payments, or something else. There are hundreds of available payment gateways, including many that gateways that specialize in serving particular countries.

Let's take a look at some of these.

- Click on "Payments" from the menu.

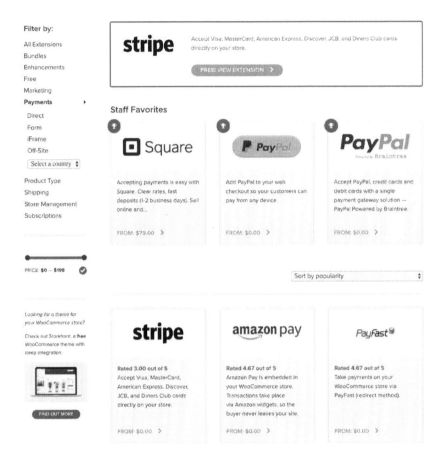

Here we can see all of the official payment gateways for WooCommerce. You'll see a few staff picks and then the list of gateways. You'll also notice that the prices range from $0-100. WooCommerce has done an awesome job partnering with payment gateways to build these extensions, which is how they can offer them to you for $0.

I do highly recommend you stay with Stripe. It's one of the best gateways and I've only had good support experiences with them. However, if you need to setup something different, here you can filter by type of gateway or even filter by country, which is super helpful.

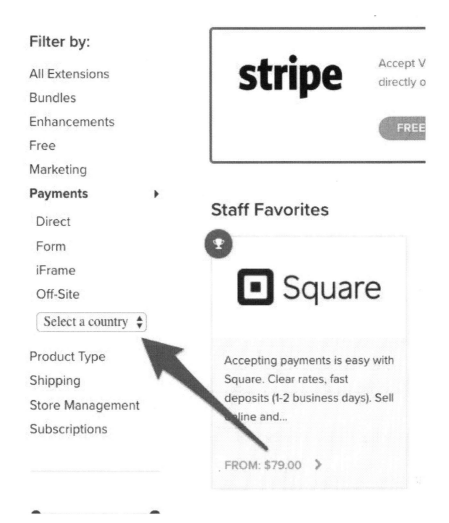

Filter by:

All Extensions

Bundles

Enhancements

Free

Marketing

Payments ▶

Direct

Form

iFrame

Off-Site

Select a country ⬍

Product Type

Shipping

Store Management

Subscriptions

stripe

Accept V
directly o

FREE

Staff Favorites

⬛ Square

Accepting payments is easy with
Square. Clear rates, fast
deposits (1-2 business days). Sell
online and...

FROM: $79.00 ❯

SHIPPING EXTENSIONS

Let's take a look at some of the shipping extensions for
WooCommerce.

- Click on "Shipping" from the menu.

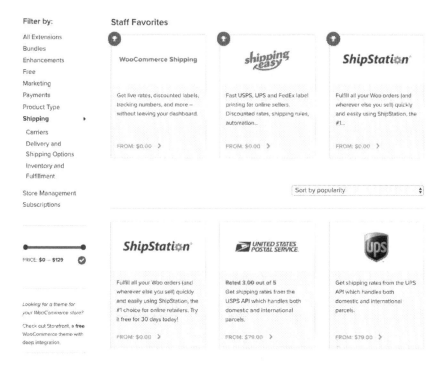

From here we can see three distinct subcategories: "Carriers," "Delivery and Shipping Options," and "Inventory and Fulfillment". Let's take a look at each of these.

- Click "Carriers".

Carriers are integrations with carriers to get live rates. We've already set up USPS through WooCommerce Services (which is called WooCommerce Shipping on this page). But if you want to integrate with FedEx, UPS, Australia Post, Canada Post, Royal Mail, etc., then you can look through this list. These extensions tend to be priced at $79.

Rated 3.00 out of 5
Get shipping rates from the USPS API which handles both domestic and international parcels.

FROM: $79.00 >

Get shipping rates from the UPS API which handles both domestic and international parcels.

FROM: $79.00 >

Get shipping rates from the FedEx API which handles both domestic and international parcels.

FROM: $79.00 >

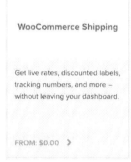

WooCommerce Shipping

Get live rates, discounted labels, tracking numbers, and more – without leaving your dashboard.

FROM: $0.00 >

Get shipping rates from the Australia Post API which handles both domestic and international parcels.

FROM: $79.00 >

Rated 1.00 out of 5
Get shipping rates from the Canada Post Ratings API which handles both domestic and international parcels.

FROM: $79.00 >

- Click "Delivery and Shipping Options".

Delivery and Shipping Options are different ways to charge users for shipping. So if you want to have a table of shipping rates, which is useful if you sell dozens, hundreds, or thousands of products at a time, you can get Table Rate Shipping.

- Click "Inventory and Fulfillment".

Inventory and Fulfillment are some of the most useful extensions in the shipping category, but they also usually have a monthly fee. These are incredibly helpful extensions to help you fulfill all of your orders from one place. Say you sell on eBay, Amazon, and your own website. All orders will be sent to one app and you can fulfill all orders from that app. You mark them as fulfilled in the app and that data is sent back to the original source.

The extensions might only cost $50-$100; however, most fulfillment companies have a monthly fee on top of that.

ENHANCEMENTS EXTENSIONS

There's one highly underrated category and that's "Enhancements".

- Click "Enhancements".

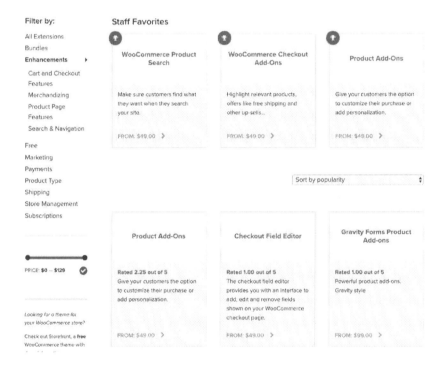

These extensions fundamentally change the way your store works.

- **Product Add-Ons:** Lets you add and upsell each product (like giftwrap or extra components).

- **Name Your Price:** Lets users enter their own price (with an optional minimum).

- **WooCommerce One Page Checkout:** Lets you list a product and the checkout on the same page. This is perfect for stores with one product.

These extensions tend to cost a little more, usually between $100-$200 but they're incredibly powerful. If you want to explore bundles, addons, or updating the cart or checkout, look through this category.

MARKETING EXTENSIONS

The last section that you should definitely look through is the Marketing category.

- Click "Marketing".

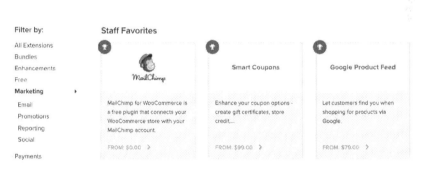

WooCommerce can connect with MailChimp, Google Products and many other services. Notice the prices of these extensions vary and range from around $0 up to $99. Most of them you'll find are about $79.

Whether you use MailChimp or another Newsletter provider, I strongly recommend you have a way to add customers to a newsletter. It's much easier to get an existing customer to buy again instead of a new customer, and newsletters let you do that.

This is a good time to mention that we're only looking at the official WooCommerce extensions. There are hundreds of WooCommerce plugins on other sites including WordPress.org.

For marketing extensions especially you might be able to find alternatives on WordPress.org.

I'm a fan of the official extensions for anything critical to your store. I always use official extensions for payment and fulfillment. And if bundles were a key component to my store, I'd use the official bundles extension.

COST OF EXTENSIONS

If you get a couple of official extensions and maybe one or two unofficial plugins, you might spend between $0-$500 per year. If you wanted to get dozens of extensions, then it might cost closer to $1,000 each year, but the vast majority of stores don't need all of that.

All things considered, this is incredibly cheap for e-commerce software when you think about all the work that goes into the security, the functionality, the planning, the streamlining, and of course the support you get for buying these extensions. Free plugins have barely any support and the official ones from WooCommerce come with live chat. That's a *huge* advantage.

Once you start buying add-ons, it becomes a bit addicting. You start wanting to buy one more to streamline this thing or that thing. As long as your store is successful, that's actually a good thing. Buying the right extensions and applying them properly is going to make your store more efficient and hopefully more profitable.

So do some research and think about your actual needs and find the appropriate extension for that need. Keep in mind WooCommerce has a 30 day refund period, so you can try it out for a week or two and then return it if you don't need it.

INSTALLING EXTENSIONS

A few extensions, like WooCommerce Services, are hosted on

WordPress.org and you install those like you would any other plugin on WordPress.org. But any of the extensions that have a yearly fee are going to have a different installation process.

When you make a purchase on WooCommerce.com, you'll be prompted to connect your store to WooCommerce.com. You can do this from your WordPress admin.

- Hover over "WooCommerce" in the main admin menu.
- Click on "Extensions".
- Click the "WooCommerce.com Subscriptions" tab.

From here we can connect our store to our account and download our extensions.

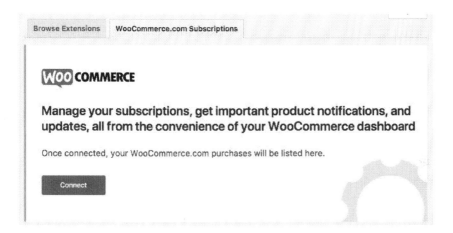

- Click "Connect".
- Agree to their terms of service and click "Allow".

And now you should be redirected back to your site, and you can download your extensions.

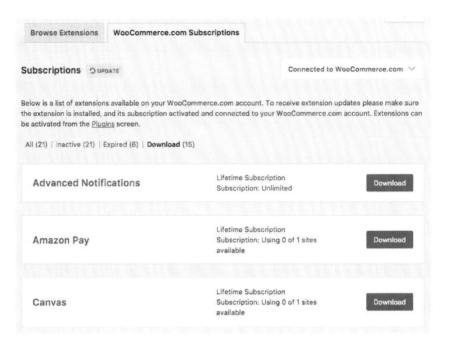

- Click "Download" to download a plugin file.
- Click "Plugins" in the main admin menu.
- Click "Upload Plugin".

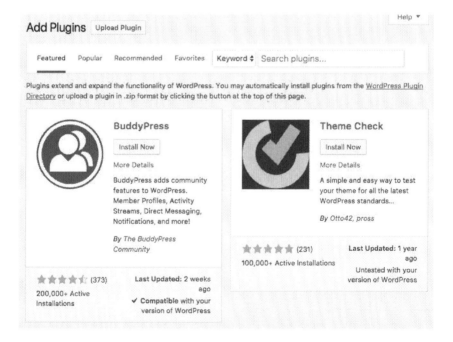

- Select the plugin that you just downloaded.
- Click "Install Now".
- Click "Activate" after it's been uploaded.

And you're up and running. It's a little more work to connect your store to WooCommerce.com than it is to install a regular WordPress.org plugin. But they're powerful, so it's worth the extra hassle.

One thing to avoid – don't manually install the plugin and not connect your store. You won't be able to get updates for WooCommerce extensions and they'll quickly go out of date and your store could eventually break. Always make sure your licenses are valid and you update your extensions.

WHAT'S NEXT?

You don't need any extensions. That's what great about WooCommerce – you don't need to pay for anything. However some of these extensions will pay for themselves by getting you more customers or keeping existing customers engaged.

You may not know what you need right now and that's fine. I recommend following the WooCommerce blog (https://woocommerce.com/blog) or subscribing to their newsletter. After consuming a few pieces of content, you'll have a better idea what functionality you may need.

In the next chapter, we'll dig more into shipping. We've gone with the default options, but you may want to explore other options.

CHAPTER 11.

WOOCOMMERCE SHIPPING EXPLAINED

During the WooCommerce onboarding wizard, we set up shipping through USPS.

In this chapter, we're going to customize our shipping settings. I'll also introduce you to a few other shipping methods you may consider using.

- In your WordPress admin, go to "WooCommerce" and then "Settings".

- Click on the "Shipping" tab, and you will see a screen like the one below.

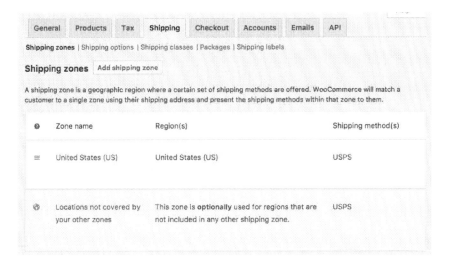

SHIPPING ZONES

The main thing you'll see on this screen are "Shipping zones". You can think of Shipping zones as a set of rules to calculate shipping costs for a particular region.

- If you want to use FedEx for every country, you only need one shipping zone.
- If you want to use FedEx for international orders, USPS for domestic orders, and give users in your state the ability to pick up an order in person, you'll need three shipping zones.

We already have domestic and international (it's called "Locations not covered by your other zones" in WooCommerce) shipping zones. Let's add one shipping zone for local orders.

- Click the "Add shipping zone" button, and you'll see a screen like the one below.

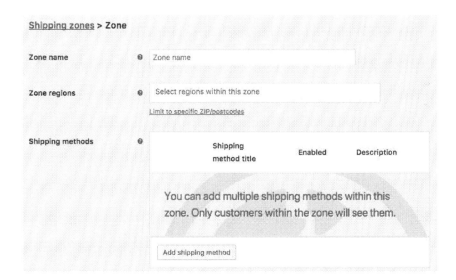

- Type "Local" as the Zone name.
- Type in your region and pick one of the suggestions.
- And then click "Add shipping method".

We want to add both USPS and local pickup.

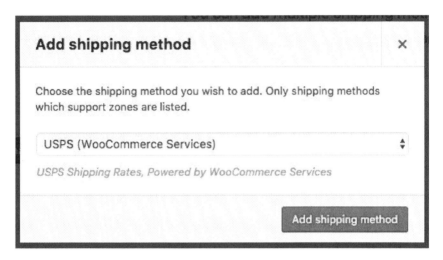

- Select "USPS (WooCommerce Services)".
- Click "Add shipping method".

You should now see the shipping method enabled under your new zone.

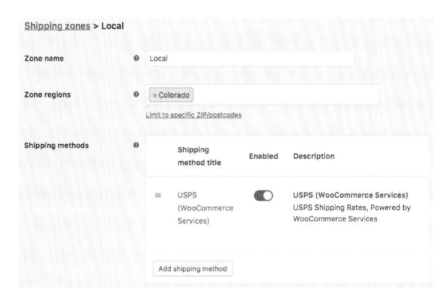

We could edit the shipping method right now. But I like to add all of my shipping methods and then go back and edit them. Let's add a shipping method so people can pick up their order at the store.

- Click "Add shipping method".
- Select "Local pickup".

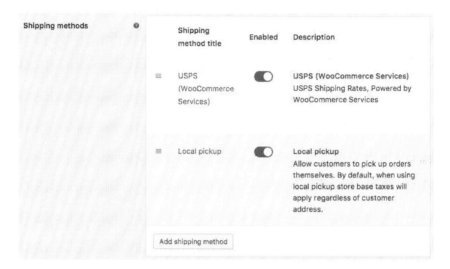

Once you're happy with your zone and the shipping methods, let's save everything.

- Click "Save changes" at the bottom of the page.

Note: If "Save changes" is greyed out and you can't click it, then rearrange the shipping methods to move Local Pickup on top and then move it down again. That should reenable the Save changes button.

- Click "Shipping zones".

Shipping zones `Add shipping zone`

A shipping zone is a geographic region where a certain set of shipping methods are offered. WooCommerce will match a customer to a single zone using their shipping address and present the shipping methods within that zone to them.

	Zone name	Region(s)	Shipping method(s)
☰	United States (US)	United States (US)	USPS
☰	Local	Colorado	Local pickup, USPS (WooCommerce Services)
⚙	Locations not covered by your other zones	This zone is **optionally** used for regions that are not included in any other shipping zone.	USPS

We've created a shipping zone and added two shipping methods to it. You can do this as many or as few times as you need. Each shipping zone has its own rules that you can configure. If you have really complex shipping methods, you can spend of lot of time setting up these zones. However, since each one needs to be configured separately, I recommend configuring as few as you need.

PACKAGES

If you use USPS or some other shipping provider, you'll need to have a list of packages that your store uses. WooCommerce automatically tries to pack all of your items into the fewest number of boxes possible and then sends those boxes to the shipping provider for a quote.

For you to get accurate rates, you'll need to have accurate package sizes as well as dimensions for each of your products.

Let's see what packages we have available for our store.

- Click "Packages" from the top menu, and you should see a screen like the one below.

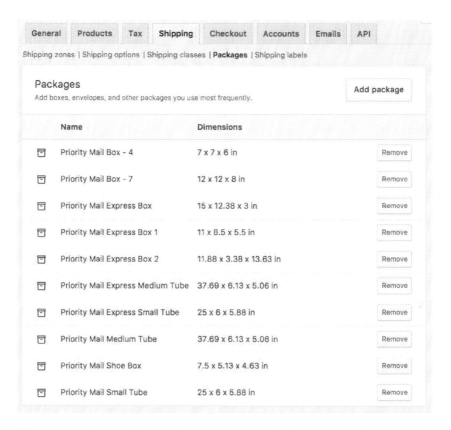

These packages have been imported from WooCommerce Services. If you use USPS, you can buy these boxes at the Post Office, which is a huge time saver. What I recommend is buying a few of these boxes and seeing which ones work well for your products (and multiples of your products).

Since Purpleville mostly sells shirts, I'm going to see which USPS boxes work best for me. You may want to look at the USPS website to see other boxes you can add: http://ostra.in/woo-usps.

If the t-shirts are pretty thin, we can probably pack them in a padded envelope instead of a box. This should save us some money since the envelopes tend to cost less than boxes. Of course, WooCommerce is smart enough to know when t-shirts won't fit in the envelope and will instead pack them in a box.

Now that we found an envelope we want to use, let's add it to our Packages.

- Click "Add package".
- Type in the dimensions of the package.
- Type in the weight of the package.
- Click "Add package".

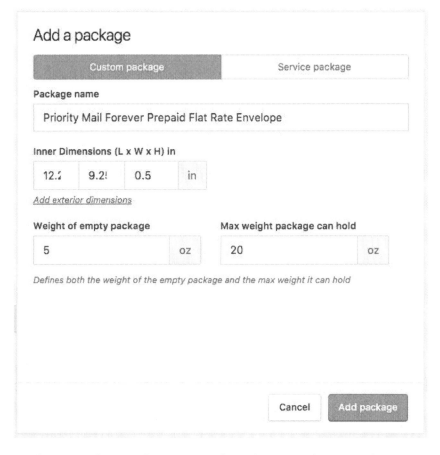

And now we're good to go. We found an envelope on the USPS site. We added it to our store and as long as our products fit in this package, WooCommerce will automatically use it for us.

One shipping method we haven't covered yet is Free Shipping.

- From the "Shipping zones" screen.

- Click one of the shipping zones that you have set up. Free Shipping must be added to each zone individually, so you do need to be editing a single zone.

- Click the "Add shipping method" button:

- Select "Free shipping".

- Click the blue "Add shipping method" button.

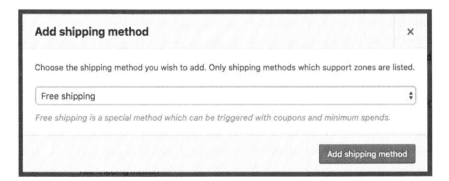

You should now see Free shipping listed with our other shipping methods. Let's configure it.

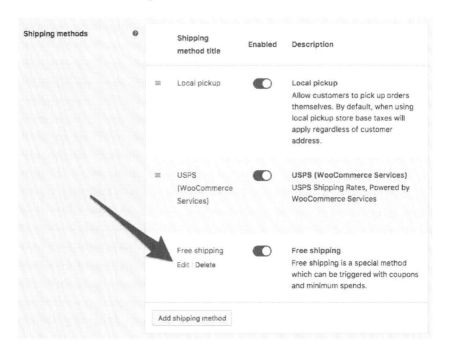

- Hover over "Free shipping".
- Click "Edit" and you should see a screen like the one below.

We could leave everything as is so that free shipping is available for every single order. However, we could lose money on smaller orders where all of our margin is eaten up by shipping.

What we want to do is to offer *unlockable free shipping*. This means that free shipping will be unlocked under certain conditions. Users don't mind paying a certain amount extra to get something free. This let's us give something awesome to our customers without breaking our business.

The trick is to figure out how much users spend on a typical order (this is called Average Order Value (AOV)). Then we need to set the unlockable free shipping price just above that.

Let's imagine that in our store the cheapest product is $20. We could set unlockable free shipping at $40 so users have to buy at least two items to get free shipping. You can set whatever makes sense for your store, and you can always made adjustments as you learn more about your customers.

- Under "Free shipping requires..." select "A minimum order amount".
- Then type in your "Minimum order amount".
- Click "Save changes".

And now you have unlockable free shipping. The image below shows how free shipping will appear to a customer during the checkout process:

Cart

Product	Price	Quantity	Total
✕ Dinosaurs Are Awesome T-Shirt	$25.00	2	$50.00

Coupon code	**Apply coupon**		Update cart

Cart totals

Subtotal	$50.00
Shipping	● Free shipping ○ Local pickup 🚚 Calculate shipping
Tax	$2.00
Total	$52.00

Proceed to checkout →

Please note that if you aren't seeing the shipping methods you expect, you might be matching the wrong shipping zone. Always put the most specific shipping zone above a more generic zone. For example, in the image below, I have listed "Colorado" above "United States" because it is the more specific of the two shipping zones.

Shipping zones | Add shipping zone

A shipping zone is a geographic region where a certain set of shipping methods are offered. WooCommerce will match a customer to a single zone using their shipping address and present the shipping methods within that zone to them.

	Zone name	Region(s)	Shipping method(s)
☰	Local	Colorado	Free shipping, Local pickup, USPS (WooCommerce Services)
☰	United States (US)	United States (US)	USPS
⊘	Locations not covered by your other zones	This zone is **optionally** used for regions that are not included in any other shipping zone.	USPS

OTHER SHIPPING METHODS

In our example, I used USPS and Local Pickup because they're easy to set up and really powerful. There are other shipping methods you can use.

Flat Rate is built into WooCommerce and is useful when you can't use a live shipping method like USPS.

For "Flat Rate" you charge a single fee regardless of distance or weight. Then you can modify it based on the number of items. So you could have a fee of $10 per order, plus $2 per item.

Note: if you want to know how to create a formula for Flat rate hover over the "?" character next to the field.

And of course there are many other shipping providers for other countries, including the Royal Post and Canada Post. You can view all of these at http://ostra.in/woo-shipping.

You'll need to pay a small amount for these shipping extensions, and you'll likely have to sign up for an account with your shipping provider. These extensions save you so much time and give you very accurate shipping costs, so I always recommend them.

WHAT'S NEXT?

The default options for shipping are great for a new store owner. But if you want to do anything with shipping, you have to start exploring shipping zones and the different shipping methods available to you. You should have a pretty good grasp of that now.

In the next chapter, we'll make sure we're collecting the right amount of taxes when someone checks out.

CHAPTER 12.

WOOCOMMERCE TAXES EXPLAINED

Welcome to one of the most complex chapters in the book.

We're going to try to explain everything in plain English, but there's no getting around the fact that taxes are a headache.

So, sit down in a comfortable chair and make yourself a strong cup of coffee. Let's explore how taxes work in WooCommerce.

E-COMMERCE AND SALES TAX

There's really only one kind of tax that e-commerce stores charge: sales tax.

Sales tax rates are different in every country. For example, if we run our company from Florida, we need to collect 6% sales tax. In California, the sales tax is 8.25%. In the UK, sales tax is 17.5%. In Spain it is 18% and in Denmark the rate is 25%.

The name also changes from country to country. In many European countries, the sales tax is called VAT (Value Added Tax). In Canada and Australia, the sales tax is called GST (Goods and Services Tax). In Japan, sales tax is known as a consumption tax.

The name of the tax, the rate, and the surrounding rules, will be different depending on where you are.

But, at the end of the day, we're all talking about the same thing. If you run an e-commerce store, you may well need to collect sales tax from your customers.

That's what this chapter is about. How do we calculate the right amount of sales tax to add to different transactions?

WOOCOMMERCE AND TAXES

When we installed WooCommerce at the beginning of the book, we enabled Automated Taxes, which is a free service from WooCommerce Services.

This service automatically sets up our tax collection for us, which can make life much, much easier.

However, before we get further, I want to encourage you to find out your legal obligations regarding taxes. Tax law varies wildly from place to place, and if you get it wrong, you are going to be in quite a mess. You will want to look at federal government taxes, state taxes, city taxes, and county taxes to find out what you need to tax and what you don't. The Automated Taxes from WooCommerce services should do this for you – but you still want to have everything checked by an expert.

This is particularly true if you have a business presence in multiple locations.

You may have heard the term nexus before. It doesn't come up often since it's a tax term – but it's key to understanding tax collection.

Nexus is any place where you have a business presence.

Each region (state, country, municipality) may define a business presence a little differently, but it's usually an employee, a storefront, a warehouse, or maybe even an affiliate. You can confirm with a tax professional where you have nexus.

For each region where you have nexus, you'll have to collect taxes. And you'll need to figure out the rate for each of those locations.

We set up Automated Taxes through WooCommerce Services at the beginning of this book. The Automated Taxes feature is incredibly powerful. But at the moment there is one limitation. It only works with one location. If you have more than one location, you'll need to figure out your own tax rates.

ENABLING TAXES

- Go to "WooCommerce" then "Settings" and then "General".
- Check to "Enable taxes and tax calculations".
- Click "Save changes".

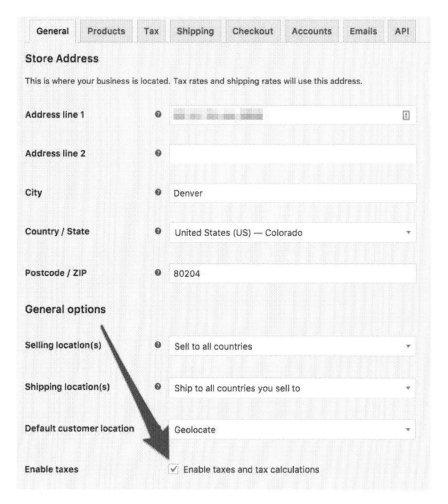

- After doing this, you should now be able to see the "Tax" tab which contains all the key tax settings.

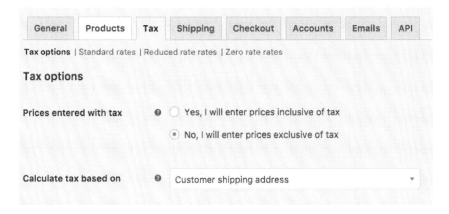

Now that taxes are enabled we can tweak some of the settings.

One of the terms you'll see here are "inclusive of tax" or "exclusive of tax":

- **Inclusive**: the prices listed on your site include tax.
- **Exclusive**: prices don't include tax and you find out at checkout what the taxes will be.

If you're in Europe, you probably use inclusive pricing. If you're in the United States, we use exclusive pricing. Since we're using the example of a US-based store, let's use the following settings:

- Select "No, I will enter prices exclusive of tax".
- Calculate Tax Based On: Choose "Customer shipping address" to determine taxes.

For "Display Prices in the Shop" and "Display Prices During Cart and Checkout," you have the option to include or exclude tax. You would want this to reflect what you set earlier in the settings.

- Set both to "Excluding tax".
- Save the changes.

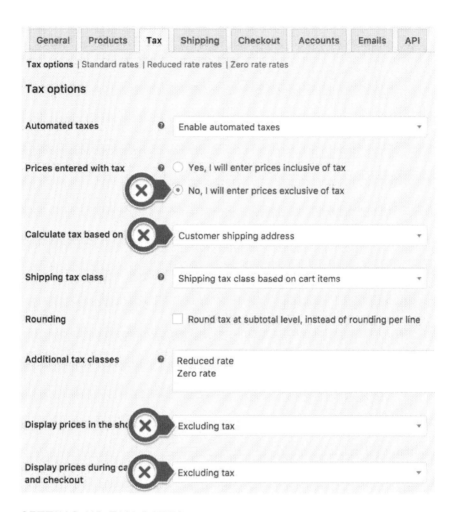

SETTING UP TAX RATES

Now let's take a look at configuring tax rates. We'll start with "Standard Rates".

- Click "Standard Rates".

You are going to want to know the alpha-2 country codes. You'll see there is a "See here" link that will take you to Wikipedia so you can view them.

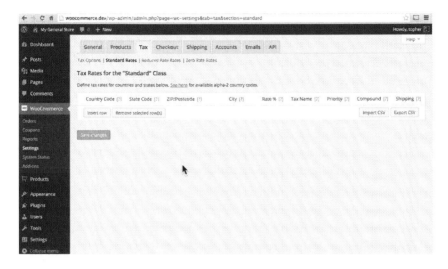

Let's insert a tax rate.

- Click "Insert Row" to get started.

Now in the US we don't have a federal tax rate for online purchases – we tend to have state rates. So we're going to add a tax rate for Colorado, where our store is based.

- **Country Code:** US

- **State Code:** CO (the state code for Colorado)

- **ZIP/Postcode:** Leave blank.

- **City:** Again, leave blank.

- **Rate:** 4%

- **Tax Name:** CO Tax

- **Priority:** Leave as 1, this shows the order they render.

- **Compound:** Compound means that your other taxes could be taxed. Let's leave this off.
- **Shipping:** Let's enable this since shipping can be taxed.
- Click "Save changes".

Note: This is an *example* rate. If you're in Colorado, you'll want to work with a tax professional to find the actual rate.

- Let's see how this works on the front-end. I have a cart here with $100 of product with $8.50 in shipping. With a state tax of 4% WooCommerce correctly adds a $4.34 tax.

Cart totals

Subtotal	$100.00
Shipping	Priority Mail: $8.50 🚚 Calculate shipping
CO Tax	$4.34
Total	$112.84

We added just one rate. You'll need to repeat this process for every place you have nexus.

TAX PRIORITY

I do want to highlight one area new store owners sometimes get stuck and that's the *priority* of the rate. You want to try to keep all similar types of rates on the same priority because only one tax from each priority level will match.

Meaning if you have nexus in Colorado and Utah and if both state tax rates have the same priority, we guarantee only one will match.

The mistake many new users make is setting a municipality and county rate to the same priority. Only one will match when you actually want both tax rates to apply and add together. If you want tax rates to apply and add together, make sure they have different priorities. A simple trick is to set country rates to 1, state rates to 2, county / zip code rates to 3, and municipality rates to 4. That way your tax rates should overlap and apply as needed.

IMPORTING RATES

If you're working with a tax professional to figure out your rates, you can make your job easier by importing and exporting rates. This reduces the risk of human error. If you only have one tax rate, you probably don't need to import / export – just be very careful when typing in the rate details.

If you're working with more than one rate, you'll probably want to import your rates just to make sure you don't have a critical typo. A trick whenever you use CSV files is to first export the file so all of the fields are in the right place.

• Click "Export CSV".

Give the file to your tax professional to fill out. When you get it back, you can import the rates.

- Click "Import CSV".
- Select your delimiter (it should remain as a comma).
- Click "Upload file and import".
- Select your file in the popup.

Now you should have a set of imported rates.

ADDITIONAL TAX CLASSES

Most stores are going to be just fine with the standard tax rates. But some stores sell products with additional taxes. Products like alcohol and cigarettes have special (aka very high) tax rates.

You can create special tax classes for products like these and tax those products at a higher rate than your other products. Only do this if you have a tax professional tell you that you have to. Otherwise, you'll want to use the standard rates.

If you want to add an additional tax class, you would simply add it into the "Additional Tax Classes" box on its own line.

- Add an "Additional tax class" called "Alcohol rate".
- Click "Save changes".

Up at the top you will see that I now have an "Alcohol rate rates" link, and that is because we included it in the "Additional tax classes" box. If I were to remove it and then save it, you would see that change reflected instantly.

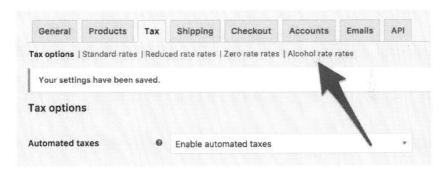

Now you can click into that rate and add tax rates as we did earlier in this chapter.

TAX OPTIONS FOR INDIVIDUAL PRODUCTS

There are also some options within individual products that I want to show you.

- Go to "Products" and select your product.

- Scroll down, and you will see that you can set "Tax status" and "Tax class" here.

So within a specific product, you can change the taxes.

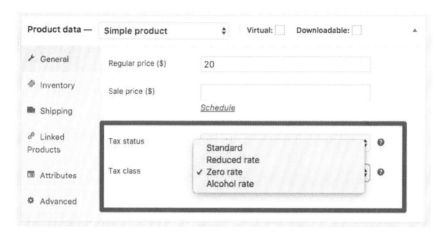

If you had a product that is tax free, you can set the "Tax class" to "Zero rate". Or if you had a product with a unique rate, you can set it to the name of that rate.

I would like to remind you that the most important part of all of this is finding out your responsibility with taxes. Consult a tax professional to see what tax rates you should use.

WHAT'S NEXT?

You know what's great? Not going to jail. By collecting taxes with WooCommerce, you can write a check to the government and not go to jail.

In all seriousness, with a good accountant and/or book keeper, collecting and remitting taxes is not too hard. And we can setup the WooCommerce tax collection in just a couple clicks.

Now that we've covered our tax liabilities, let's start to look into marketing. We're going to add coupons and see how we can use them to promote our store.

CHAPTER 13.

WOOCOMMERCE COUPONS EXPLAINED

Coupons are a core feature of any eCommerce site.

Coupons are often a fundamental part of the marketing strategy for stores.

You may want to create a holiday discount, a discount code for first time customers, or a discount code just for a special audience such as your newsletter or a podcast.

In this chapter, we're going to look at how to set up coupons in WooCommerce.

CREATING YOUR FIRST COUPON

The example we're going to use for coupons is linked to the launch of our Purpleville store. We're going to offer a $20 discount for everyone who buys at least $75 worth or products.

- Log in to your WordPress site. Go to "WooCommerce" and then "Coupons".

- If this is your first time here, you'll see a blank page.

- Click "Create your first coupon".

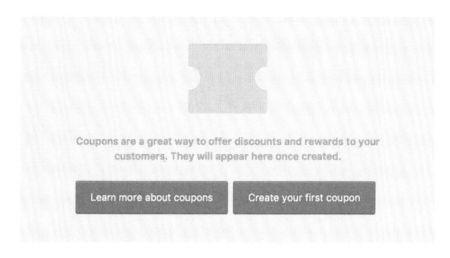

Coupons are a great way to offer discounts and rewards to your customers. They will appear here once created.

[Learn more about coupons] [Create your first coupon]

After the page loads, we'll see all of the fields we need to fill out.

First, we need to add the Coupon code, which is what the user has to enter to apply the coupon.

- Type in a name into the "Coupon Code" field. I'll enter "purpevillelaunch".

- Enter a description for the coupon. This is just for your purposes. So you can enter a description to remind yourself and anyone else what this coupon is used for. I'll add "This 20% discount will be for the launch of the Purpleville store".

Add new coupon

purpevillelaunch

This 20% discount will be for the launch of the Purpleville store

Now we need to enter a discount. There are a few different types of discounts:

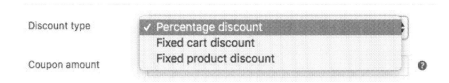

What's the difference between these coupon types? Let's imagine a cart contains two Dinosaur T-shirts and two Plain T-shirts for $20 each. The cart total will be $80. Here are different ways the coupons can impact this order:

- **Percentage discount**: A coupon for 10% would result in savings of of $8.

- **Fixed cart discount**: A coupon for $20 would result in savings of of $20.

- **Fixed product discount:** This gives the customer a flat discount on only some products. So, a coupon for $5 might only apply to Dinosaur T-shirts. This would result in savings of $10.

For our store, I want to offer a really good discount. So I'm going to offer a $20 Fixed cart discount:

- Set "Discount type" to "Fixed cart discount".

- Set "Coupon amount" to "20".

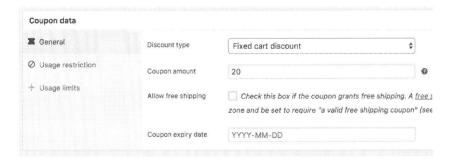

Now we need to add our restrictions:

- Click the "Usage restriction" tab.

- Set the "Minimum spend" to 75 if you want to make sure people don't get the discount for only spending a few dollars.

- Enable "Individual use only" to make sure it isn't combined with any other coupons.

Our coupon is pretty great. We just want to add a few more restrictions. If we don't, users can use this coupon over and over again.

- Click the "Usage limits" tab.

- Under "Usage limit per user" enter "1". This way our new customers can only use the coupon once.

- Click "Publish".

- The coupon is live on the site and we can test it ourselves to make sure it works.

		Product	Price	Quantity	Total
⊗	👕	Dinosaur T-Shirt	$20.00	6	$120.00

Coupon code	Apply coupon		Update cart

Cart totals

Subtotal	$120.00
Coupon: purpevillelaunch	-$20.00 [Remove]
Total	$100.00

It is possible to track how which coupons are most successful:

- In your WordPress admin area, go to "WooCommerce" and then "Reports".

- Click "Orders" and then "Coupons by date".

- You'll see a graphic report that shows how often each coupon has been used.

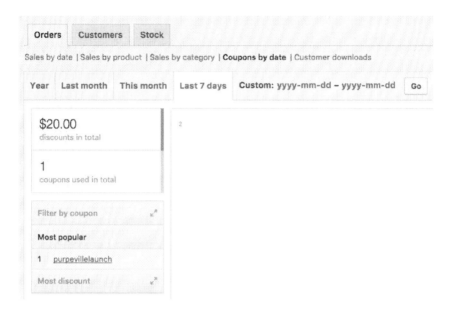

GOING FURTHER WITH COUPONS

We created a simple launch coupon in this chapter. Your store may well need a more sophisticated coupon strategy. You can look into discounts on specific products, product categories, or even offer free shipping.

The trick with coupons is to make sure that someone can't use a coupon meant for 50% off a $10 item on a $1,000 item. Be very specific with how you create your coupons to make sure you don't let someone use coupons in an unintentional way. That way you can avoid having to eat the cost or refunding the order and possibly angering the customer.

One plugin we recommend is WooCommerce Extended Coupon Features.

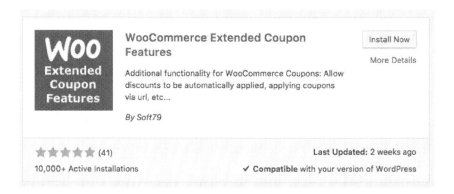

This will add extra features directly into the default WooCommerce Coupons area. After installing the plugin, go and edit a coupon. You will see a new "Checkout" area on the left-hand side. This allows you to create coupons that apply to specific customers or user roles. You can also create coupons for customers who use a specific shipping method or payment method.

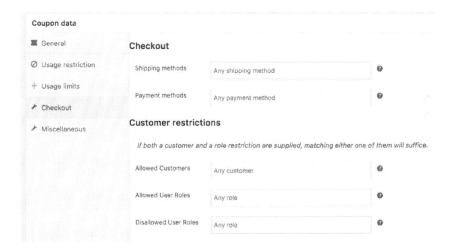

Under the "Miscellaneous" tab, you'll have the option to automatically add the coupon to the users account, if the criteria are met. This is a user-friendly feature because customers do often forget to enter a coupon, or they will type it incorrectly.

WHAT'S NEXT?

Coupons let us promote our store and they also let us track the progress of those campaigns (using the coupon reports). They're a very useful marketing tool that you want to add to your tool-belt.

Next up we'll learn how to manage orders on your store. We'll process the orders, issue refunds, and print shipping labels.

CHAPTER 14.

WOOCOMMERCE ORDER MANAGEMENT EXPLAINED

As a store owner one of the things you'll need to do on a daily basis is review new orders, pack the goods, and send them out. You may also from time to time track down a mistake that was made. Even if you're perfect, you'll still have to fulfill refunds from time to time.

In this chapter, we are going to take a look at the order system within WooCommerce. We'll start by covering how to fulfill orders, then we'll go over how to refund orders, and then how you track down an issue using order notes.

- In your WordPress admin area, click "WooCommerce".

- Here you can see that we have few orders. If you don't have any here, you can go through the checkout yourself and make some test orders.

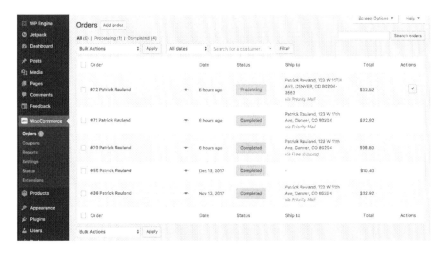

EXPLORING THE ORDER PAGE

On this page, we see a list of orders and their details. We see customer information, the date, the status, shipping address, a total, and a list of actions we can take.

I've already completed some of these orders. If you're selling virtual products (products that don't require shipping), they should automatically be completed. But as a new store owner, one of the most useful things you can do is filter the orders to only see the ones you need to work on.

We can look for the Processing status. But if we have pages of orders, that can still be confusing. You might click into the wrong order. Instead it's best to filter the orders.

- Click "Processing" above the list of orders.

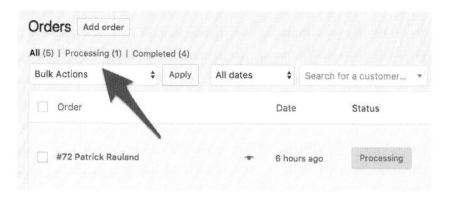

Note: You'll only see "Processing" if there are orders with that status. If you don't have orders, or they're all a different status, you won't see that option.

Alright, now we're only looking at the orders we need to fulfill today. To accomplish that we need to look into each order, pack the items into boxes, and then ship those boxes. Let's start that.

- Click the "eye" icon to preview the order, and you'll see a screen like the one below.

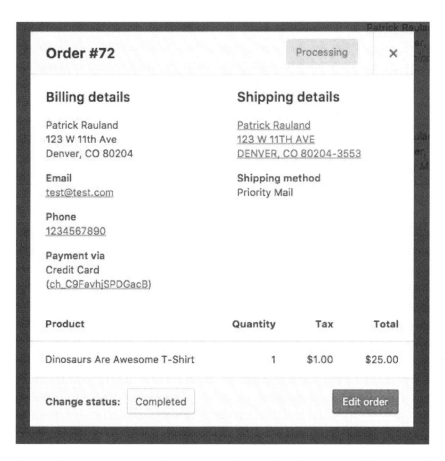

From here we can see a list of products, the shipping address, and the shipping method. Once we pack all of the items and get them ready to go, we can mark the order as "Completed".

That's the basics. And this works great for free shipping or flat rate shipping. Right now the order preview doesn't let you print shipping labels. For that we'll have to open a separate page.

- Close the preview by clicking on the "X".
- Click an order number from the list of orders.

This opens the order detail page. From here we can do all sorts of things like refund the order, edit the products, resend emails, as well as see the status and history of the order.

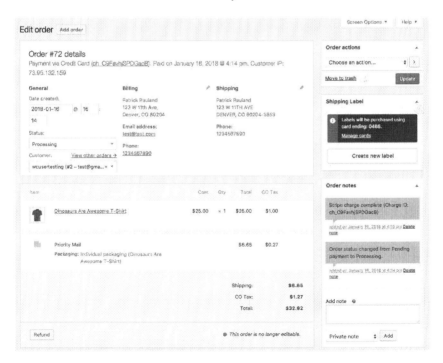

Let's purchase that shipping label so we can just drop the package off at the post office.

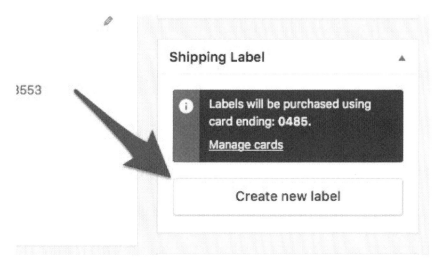

If you have a credit card set up, you should see a box similar to this. Otherwise in it's place you'll see a notice about setting up payment.

- Click "Create new label".

Follow the prompts to print out the label. USPS will let you know if the address looks like a real address. If not, they'll prompt you to edit it (and give you suggestions on how to do so). When you've gone through their prompts, you should see a final price.

Note: If you aren't using USPS or JetPack Services, you'll have a different interface and you might not be able to buy labels directly from the admin. Each shipping carrier will work differently.

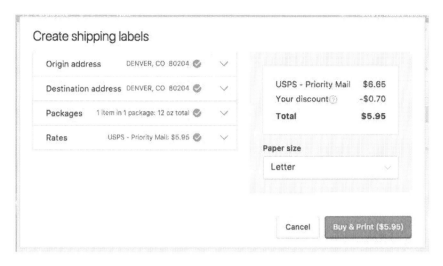

- Click "Buy & Print".

You should be able to see the label and print it. Your order should automatically be changed from "Processing" to "Completed". You just need to pack the box and drop it off at the post office.

ISSUING REFUNDS FOR ORDERS

One other thing you'll have to do as a store owner is handle refunds. With most payment gateways, including Stripe, this is very easy to do. You can refund any order that's accepted payment. That's any order that's processing or completed.

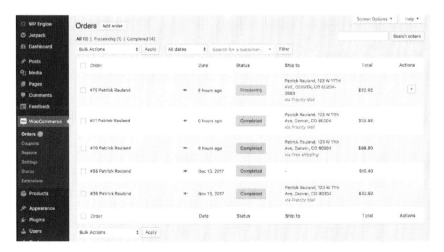

- Start at the "Orders" screen in WooCommerce.

- Click into an order.

- Scroll down to the "Refund" button.

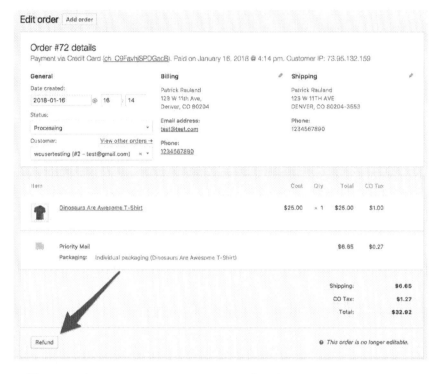

- Type in the amount you want to refund.

- Type in a reason.

Restock refunded items:	☑
Amount already refunded:	-$0.00
Total available to refund:	$32.92
Refund amount:	32.92
❷ Reason for ____nd (optional):	customer reques

Refund $32.92 manually | Refund $32.92 via Stripe

The reason for a refund is recorded in WooCommerce. So it's worth taking the extra two seconds to type something in here. It doesn't have to be super detailed. Even something like "customer request" is helpful a few years down the line just to see where your refunds are coming from.

• Click the "Refund" button for your gateway.

If you do refund through your gateway, it's automatically returning their money via your gateway. If you click the manual button, it only marks the order as refunded and you still have to return the money manually through your gateway. Only do this if your gateway doesn't support automatic refunds. This is one more reason to use Stripe.

When you're done, the order will be marked as "Refunded".

Order		Date	Status
#72 Patrick Rauland		6 hours ago	Processing
#71 Patrick Rauland		6 hours ago	Completed
#70 Patrick Rauland		6 hours ago	Refunded
#55 Patrick Rauland		Dec 13, 2017	Completed
#36 Patrick Rauland		Nov 13, 2017	Completed

ADDING ORDER NOTES

Whether you're working for yourself or with people, you'll at some point have to track something that went awry. Maybe a customer sent in a request to change the color of a t-shirt, or they had issues paying and they sent you a manual Paypal payment. When you have dozens or hundreds of orders, you'll lose track of these changes. That's when you'll need to look through a log.

On the order details page are "Order notes". Notes are automatically generated and you can manually add any note you want. For example, when payment is successful we see an order note. If we refunded the order, we'd see another order note.

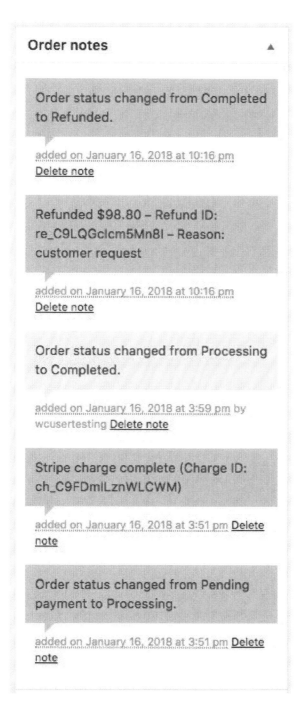

Order notes ▲

Order status changed from Completed to Refunded.

added on January 16, 2018 at 10:16 pm
Delete note

Refunded $98.80 – Refund ID: re_C9LQGcIcm5Mn8I – Reason: customer request

added on January 16, 2018 at 10:16 pm
Delete note

Order status changed from Processing to Completed.

added on January 16, 2018 at 3:59 pm by wcusertesting Delete note

Stripe charge complete (Charge ID: ch_C9FDmILznWLCWM)

added on January 16, 2018 at 3:51 pm Delete note

Order status changed from Pending payment to Processing.

added on January 16, 2018 at 3:51 pm Delete note

All important actions with an order will be logged here. So if something goes wonky – like a customer says they paid but the order isn't marked as such – you can come to the order notes to see exactly what happened.

Let's say a customer accidentally paid with their business PayPal account instead of their personal account and they send an email immediately after ordering trying to correct the situation. We could add this to the log. At the bottom of the log, you'll see a spot to add a note.

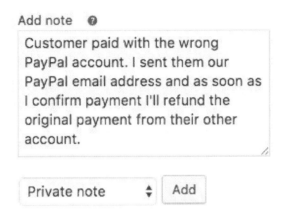

- Type a note in the note field and click "Add".

You can also change the status of the note from "Private note" to "Note to customer" and it will be logged as well as sent to the customer. I personally prefer writing concise notes on each order and writing notes to customers with language appropriate for humans, so I rarely use this option. But it's there if you want it.

WHAT'S NEXT?

Now that you know how to fulfill orders, refund orders, and track down anything that could have gone wrong, it's time to look at some of stats that WooCommerce collects. In the next chapter, we'll look at the reports you can find in WooCommerce.

CHAPTER 15.

WOOCOMMERCE REPORTS EXPLAINED

Once you start making sales, you can start looking through all of the data that WooCommerce collects.

In the beginning there isn't a ton of data, but the longer your store is around the more useful that data is. You'll learn how profitable some customers are and which products are the most popular. You'll be able to monitor coupon usage and see which marketing campaigns are working.

In this chapter, we are going to take a look at reports in WooCommerce.

ORDERS REPORT

Viewing all of your orders is one of the more useful reports. It's a quick check on the health of your store.

- In your admin, go to "WooCommerce" then "Reports".

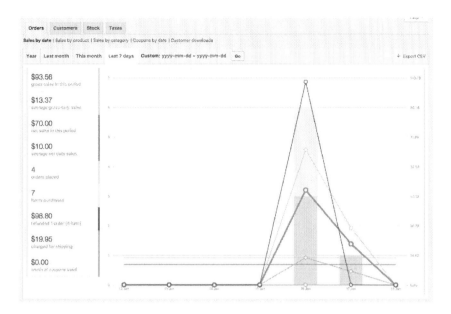

You'll notice the graph is quite complex. WooCommerce lays a bunch of data together on one graph and they use different scales, which can be confusing.

- Hover your mouse over one of the labels on the left.

Notice that the label itself will change to purple as will one of the items in the graph. This is the easiest way to understand which item in the graph is correlated with the label on the left.

GROWTH OVER METRICS

Store owners always ask me is my {insert metric here} good? And the answer is, it depends on *your* store. There is no such thing as a good revenue metric, or a good number of orders.

A friend of mine sells women's clothing which is fairly cheap. It took them some time to build solid revenue numbers. Another friend sold high end sunglasses that cost $80 to $160. They were immediately able to get their revenue going. Each store is different.

What you want to focus on is growth. Never compare yourself to another store – but do compare yourself to past versions of yourself.

Compare this week's revenue to last week's revenue, last month's revenue, or last year's revenue. That's the best way to measure any metric in your store.

TAXES

One of the most useful reports in WooCommerce is the taxes

graph, because it tells you exactly how much money you should set aside in your taxes account.

- Click the "Taxes" tab.
- You can see a list of your tax obligations – in this case I have just one.

This is incredibly helpful for anyone who is managing the books for your store. You need to set aside this money for taxes, and with reports like this, you know exactly how much to set aside.

EXPORTING DATA

All of these reports are exportable via CSV. I rarely want to export my data but if I have to export my data, I don't want to be locked in. You always want the option to get your data in a CSV even if you don't plan on doing anything with it. You may need it if you ever change platforms or get audited. Or possibly your accountant may need to review it. You never know what you'll need the data for, but it's helpful to know any report can be exported into CSV.

NEXT STEPS

The reports in WooCommerce are a starting point. But if you want to learn about your customers and where they come from, I recommend you start looking into Google Analytics: https://analytics.google.com. The analytics tools from Google are a more powerful feature to track traffic to your site. If you're new to Google Analytics, try the class at https://www.ostraining.com/class/google-analytics.

If you want some WooCommerce-specific analytics, try http://metorik.com, which was started by a former employee of Automattic, who own WooCommerce.

Metorik provides more powerful reports than the WooCommerce core and you can get those reports emailed to you regularly. Metorik also offers the ability to drill down into your data and analyze specific groups of orders, customers or products.

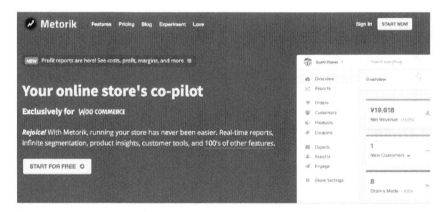

WHAT'S NEXT?

Again, the reports in WooCommerce are a great place to get started but if you're serious about learning about your customers, you'll have to upgrade to a more powerful reporting platform (like Google Analytics) at some point.

In the next chapter, we'll look at a few different ways you can manage your inventory.

CHAPTER 16.

WOOCOMMERCE INVENTORY EXPLAINED

We talked about inventory when we added our first WooCommerce products, but it's worth looking at global inventory settings so we can make them work for us.

With a little tweaking we can enable/disable stock settings entirely. We can also customize how long someone can hold stock in their cart, and we can send notifications when our stock starts running low.

ENABLING STOCK

- From the admin, click on "WooCommerce" -> "Settings" -> "Products" -> "Inventory".

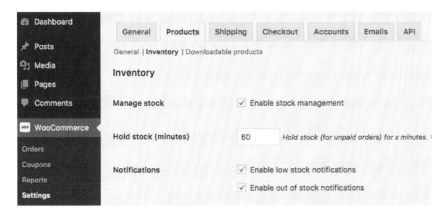

If you run a store where all of the products are digital, you probably don't even need inventory. You will always have the products available for customers. If that's the case, you can turn off the "Enable stock management" setting.

Inventory

Manage stock	☑ Enable stock management
Hold stock (minutes)	60 *Hold stock (for unpaid orders) for x minutes.*
Notifications	☑ Enable low stock notifications
	☑ Enable out of stock notifications

The "Hold stock (minutes)" setting is there to prevent multiple users from checking out at the same time. When someone adds a product to their cart, WooCommerce holds onto it to prevent someone else from coming in and buying it. However, if the customer chooses not to buy the product, you don't want to leave it in their cart forever. To solve this you can set the "Hold stock" so that after a certain amount of minutes it will release it back into your inventory. Go ahead and leave this at the default unless you have problems with people holding onto stock, in which case you'll want to lower this.

The only other setting I suggest changing is the "Low stock threshold".

Notifications	☑ Enable low stock notifications
	☑ Enable out of stock notifications
Notification recipient(s) ❷	▨▨▨▨@gmail.com
Low stock threshold ❷	2
Out of stock threshold ❷	0

WooCommerce automatically sends you an email when you're low in stock so you can reorder and not run out. This is a *very* useful notification. For most stores it takes several days to get resupplied from a supplier and it takes months to get resupplied from a manufacturer. If you sell one unit a day and it takes 30 days to get new stock in, I suggest setting the low stock notification to at least 30.

If you have no idea how fast your products sell (this is called velocity in the retail world), assume on the low side. It's better to run out of stock than spend all of your capital on products that don't sell.

Since Purpleville is going to be the best store in all of existence, I'm going to set mine to 35 to give me a few extra days of buffer. ?

- Set the "Low stock threshold" to 35.

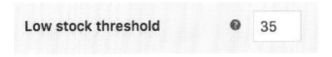

Low stock threshold ❷	35

PRODUCT LEVEL INVENTORY SETTINGS

We've looked at the site-wide inventory settings. This controls most of what we want. But there are product level settings that we can also tweak.

- Navigate to one of your products in the admin.
- Scroll down to the "Product data" tab.
- Click the "Inventory" tab.

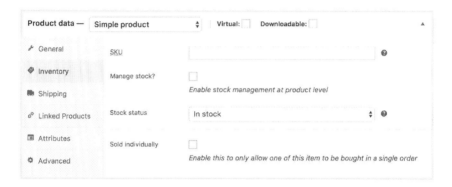

There are some really useful fields here.

- **SKU** is one of the most useful fields when you have to integrate with another system. A product's SKU is how two systems talk to each other about the same product. So if you want to have a third party system that ships products or that manages inventory, you'll need to set a SKU for each product.

- **Stock status** let's you manually mark a product "In stock," "Out of stock," or "Backorder". This will display on the front end.

- **Manage stock?** I recommend clicking this checkbox. That will make a new field, "Stock quantity," appear. Then you can enter the exact number in stock and WooCommerce will track it for you.

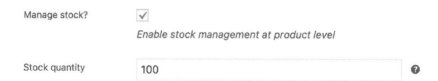

Once we've entered an SKU so we can integrate with third parties and we've set the stock level of each product, we're done. WooCommerce will manage all of our stock levels for us and notify us when we get low in inventory.

You can check which products are running low by going to "WooCommerce" -> "Reports" -> "Stock". Here you'll see a table showing which products are "Low in stock". You can click the tabs to see products that are "Out of stock" or "Most stocked".

It's also possible to make the stock data visible to customers.

- Install the plugin called WooCommerce Availablity Chart:

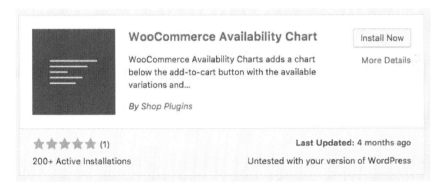

- You don't need to configure any settings for this plugin. It will automatically show your customers how many of each item are in stock. In the image below, you can see the smiley face next to "1 in stock".

Dinosaur T-Shirts

$20.00

☺ 1 in stock

Add to cart

WHAT'S NEXT?

This is a an introduction to inventory in WooCommerce. Keeping control of your inventory is one of the key challenges for anyone selling physical products and if you sell this kind of store, you'll spend a lot of time in this area of WooCommerce.

In the next chapter, let's take a look at some search engine optimization (SEO) settings that can help you bring in more traffic.

CHAPTER 17.

WOOCOMMERCE STORE OPTIMIZATION EXPLAINED

Search Engine Optimization, or SEO, is a whole subject area which has dozens of books in any given bookstore. It's the practice of getting your site to load as high as possible on a search engine results page (SERP). The general topic of SEO is too big for this book, but we did think it was important to include at least a little bit to get you started. Let's start with what WooCommerce does for you.

WooCommerce handles the technical SEO for your site. That means all of the code is written in such a way that it's as clear as possible for the search engines. And that means when a search engine thinks it's appropriate, it will show extra information in the search results.

For example, say I search for the board game "Catan".

Google will know it's a product and automatically include extra information.

- Product rating
- Number of reviews
- Price

- Target audience

- Age range

- And even related products

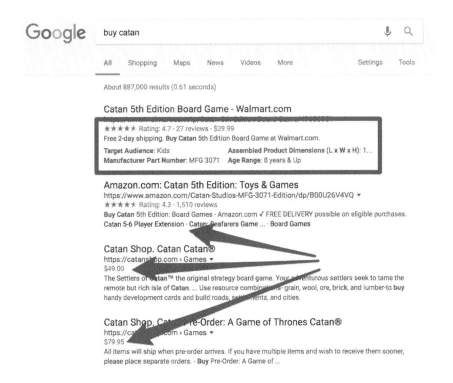

Now we as website owners don't have 100% control over what the search engines display. But we can share all of this data with search engines, and they'll display what they think is most relevant. Unlikely many shopping carts, WooCommerce handles all of that for us.

If I view the HTML source of one of our products, we'll see some information about the product. Don't worry, you don't need to know what this code says! Just understand that WooCommerce is telling search engines everything about your product in a format that they can easily digest. WooCommerce is very good at handling the technical aspects of search engine optimization.

```
696 <script type="application/ld+json">{"@context":"https:\/\/schema.org\/","@graph":
[{"@context":"https:\/\/schema.org\/","@type":"BreadcrumbList","itemListElement":
[{"@type":"ListItem","position":"1","item":{"name":"Home","@id":"http:\/\/purpleville.com"}},
{"@type":"ListItem","position":"2","item":{"name":"Clothing","@id":"http:\/\/purpleville.com\/product-
category\/clothing\/"}},{"@type":"ListItem","position":"3","item":{"name":"Dinosaurs Are Awesome T-Shirt"}}]},
{"@context":"https:\/\/schema.org\/","@type":"Product","@id":"http:\/\/puepleville.com\/product\/dinosaurs-
awesome-t-shirt\/","name":"Dinosaurs Are Awesome T-Shirt","image":"http:\/\/wcusertesting.wpengine.com\/wp-
content\/uploads\/2017\/11\/dinosaurs-are-awesome.jpg","description":"Celebrate your love of dinosaurs with
our Dinosaurs Are Awesome t-shirt. They're huge, they're lizards, and they're in our favorite movie: Jurassic
Park.","sku":"","offers":
[{"@type":"Offer","price":"25.00","priceCurrency":"USD","availability":"https:\/\/schema.org\/InStock","url":"
http:\/\/purplevle.com\/product\/dinosaurs-awesome-t-shirt\/","seller":
{"@type":"Organization","name":"Purpleville","url":"http:\/\/purpleville.com"}}]}]}}</script>
```

So WooCommerce handles the technical SEO. What do you have to do?

1. Make your site load fast.
2. Build a good structure for your site.

We'll cover how you can do both of these with WooCommerce in this chapter.

MAKING YOUR SITE LOAD FAST

Making your site load fast is a big topic and you'll hear people suggest many different solutions.

First and foremost, you want to make sure you use a good host. An excellent host, such as http://nexcess.net, will put you on a fast server. And because they know WooCommerce really well, they will optimize their servers specifically for WordPress and WooCommerce. The difference between a bad hosting company and a good hosting company can be a 300% or 400% speed boost. Nothing will speed up your site effectively if you have poor-quality hosting.

Earlier in the book we installed the Jetpack plugin. This one plugin contains many different features, including two that will speed up your site by making your images load faster. Large and slow-loading images are very common reason for sites to run sluggishly.

- Go to "Jetpack" -> "Settings" -> "Writing".
- In the "Speed up your site" section, enable both of these features:
  ◦ Server images from our servers
  ◦ Lazy load images

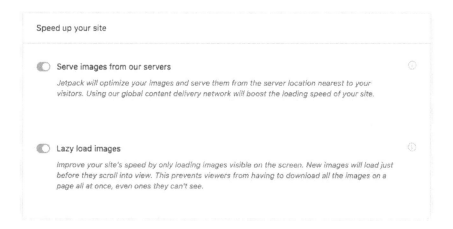

The first option is called a "CDN" or "Content Delivery Network". By default, websites are normally hosted in one location. So a website hosted in New York might feel very fast if you're sitting in Washington DC. However, it might feel very slow if you're sitting in India. The "Serve images from our servers" feature will place a copy of your images in different locations around the globe. Visitors will always get the copy of the image that's closest to them, so your site will appear to be faster. One consequence of this is that your image URLs will be from wp.com (a WordPress.com site) rather than your own domain.

The second option is a solution to slow the speed of long web pages. Normally, when a visitor arrives at a web page, all the images on the page are loaded. This can be a lot of images for a long page. In contrast, if you choose "Lazy load images," then your website will only load the images that your visitor can see. As the visitor scrolls down the page, your site will keep loading the extra images they need to see.

A free tool most stores aren't using yet is AMP (Accelerated Mobile Pages). There's a WordPress plugin for it: https://wordpress.org/plugins/amp. AMP detects your user's browser and serves them a mobile optimized page automatically. Google is behind AMP to try to make the web faster. There are rumors that Google will give an advantage to pages that have an AMP version available.

BUILDING A GOOD STRUCTURE FOR YOUR SITE

You can also focus on the structure of your site. Search engines like hierarchy. When they can't send someone to a product page, they'd like to send someone to a category page.

Here's what search engines like to see:

- Category 1
  - Product 1
  - Product 2

- Category 2

  ○ Product 3

  ○ Product 4

- Category 3

  ○ Product 5

  ○ Product 6

So if someone is searching for something that isn't clearly one of our products, we want those people to land on our category pages.

Let's optimize those pages.

- In our admin under "Products" click "Categories".

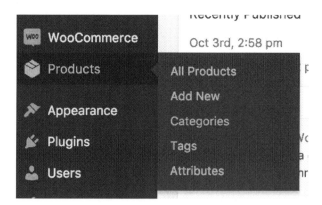

On this page we can see our existing categories and add new categories. Notice how there's nothing under the "Description" header. We're going to change that.

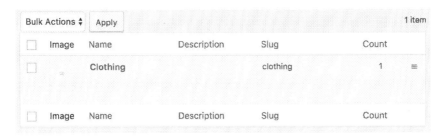

	Image	Name	Description	Slug	Count	
☐	Image	Name	Description	Slug	Count	
☐		Clothing		clothing	1	≡
☐	Image	Name	Description	Slug	Count	

Bulk Actions ⬍ Apply   1 item

- Click the title of the category to edit it.

- Once you're on the edit page, you'll see a text field for your description.

- Go ahead and describe your product category. At a minimum write a few sentences, but hopefully you can write a paragraph or two.

- Click "Update" when you're done.

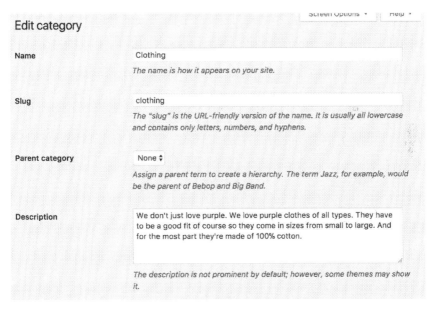

- If we go to the frontend of our site, we can navigate to our category. If you don't have a link to the category, you can go to a product page and then click on the link to the category.

Clothing

We don't just love purple. We love purple clothes of all types. They have to be a good fit of course so they come in sizes from small to large. And for the most part they're made of 100% cotton.

Default sorting ⇕   Showing all 2 results

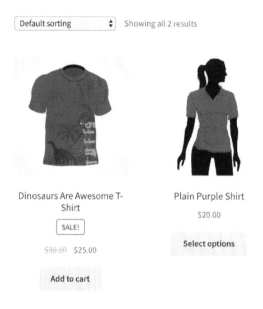

Dinosaurs Are Awesome T-Shirt

SALE!

~~$30.00~~ $25.00

Add to cart

Plain Purple Shirt

$20.00

Select options

This gives search engines like Google a little more incentive to send people to category pages instead of our home page. This is great for the user and for our business since more people will be checking out. Joost de Valk, whose plugin we are going to recommend in the next section of this chapter, is an expert on WordPress SEO. He has this to say about category pages: https://yoast.com/category-seo/.

Your category archives are more important than individual pages and posts. This is true regardless of whether your site is a blog, an e-commerce site or something else. Those archives should be the first result in the search engines. That means those archives are your most important landing pages. They should therefore also provide the best user experience.

WRITING SEO OPTIMIZED CONTENT

In the early part of this chapter, we talked about technical improvements to your website.

But, if you can't write content that visitors and search engines find interesting, then all the optimizations in the world won't help you.

Let's take a look at how you can write content that is SEO optimized. This applies to your WooCommerce product pages, plus also blog posts and other content on your site. The most popular solution in the WordPress world for that is Yoast SEO (https://yoast.com). They have a free plugin on WordPress.org that helps you write optimized content.

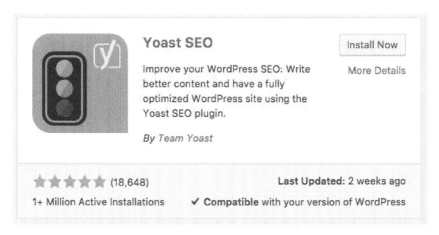

The Yoast plugin provides tools and advice you help you write optimize product descriptions. It will remind you to use your SEO keyword in your title and text, add alt tags to images, link to other pages in your site, and a lot of other SEO best practices.

- After installing Yoast SEO, go to edit one of your WooCommerce products.

- Scroll down and look for the "Yoast SEO" box under the main product description.

- Your first task is to choose a "Focus keyword" at the bottom of this box. This is the single keyword that you are optimizing your product for. The normal advice of SEO experts is that your pages should focus on a single phrase.

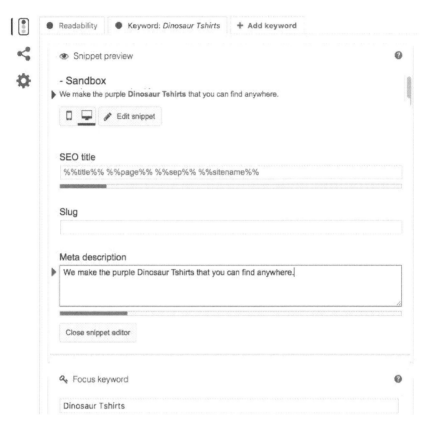

- After you enter a Focus keyword, look up to the "Publish" box.
- Here you can see a "Readability" score and an "SEO" score. Both of these boxes are currently red, which means we have work to do.

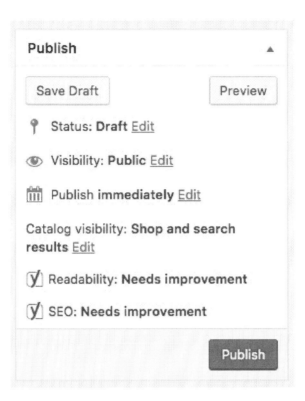

- Scroll back down to the "Yoast SEO" box, and you'll see recommendations for improving your product content. As you fix each of these issues, the red marks will turn green.

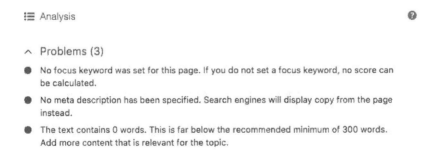

When you've finished implementing the advice from Yoast SEO, the "Publish" box will show two green check marks:

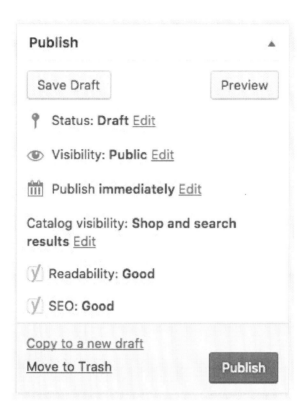

CREATING HIGH-QUALITY PRODUCT PAGES

If you have a lot of products on your WooCommerce site, it can be difficult to create consistent, high-quality product pages. With a lot of settings, its easy to forget something.

To make sure that all your WooCommerce pages meet your standards, we recommend the PublishPress plugin with the WooCommerce Checklist add-on.

- Install the free PublishPress plugin.
- Buy and install the Content Checklist http://ostra.in/ checklist and the WooCommerce Checklist from http://ostra.in/woo-check.

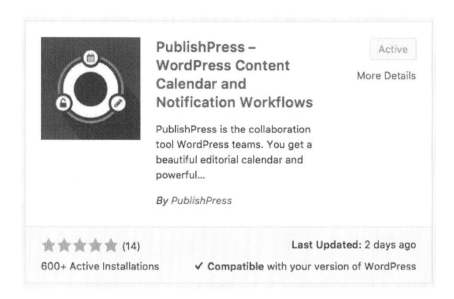

- Go to "PublishPress" -> "Settings" -> "Checklist".

- The WooCommerce Checklist doesn't appear on WooCommerce by default. You need to select the "Products" post type for use with the Checklist:

- Check the "Product" post type box.
- You can now choose all of your requirements for each WooCommerce product. You can choose the number of

categories, tags, and words. You can decide which boxes people need to check.

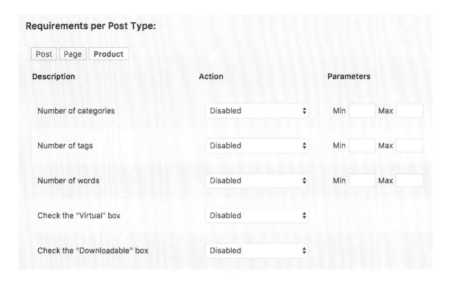

Each requirement has a certain number of options:

- **Show a sidebar message** (default): This simply shows the recommendation in the sidebar when creating a WooCommerce product.

- **Show a pop-up message**: This will display a pop-up with a warning message, but users can still publish.

- **Prevent publishing**: Users won't be able to publish if this is not complete.

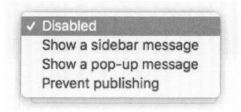

- Save the Checklist page.
- Go to edit a WooCommerce product, and view the new box in

the right sidebar. Requirements that are complete have a green check. Requirement that are incomplete have a red X.

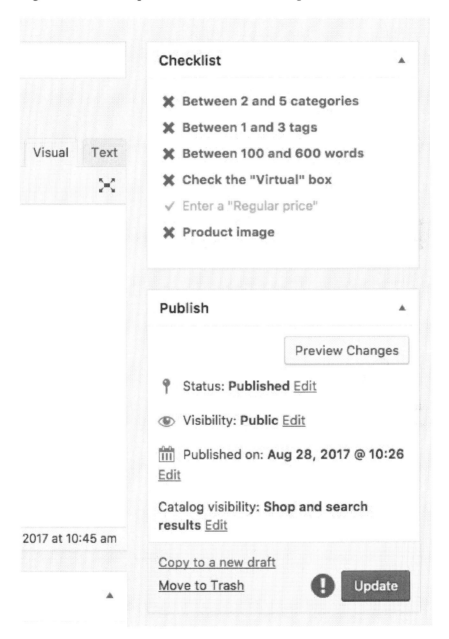

On a busy site, the WooCommerce Checklist can save you from making expensive data-entry mistakes. You can make sure that every product has a price, a title and categories. You can make sure that all your products are marked as "Downloadable" or "Virtual".

WHAT'S NEXT?

By improving the technical and content aspects of our site, we have made it easier for people to find our product in Google's search results.

In the next chapter, we'll look at how you can make your store more secure. If you're taking people's money, you need to take security very seriously.

CHAPTER 18.

WOOCOMMERCE SECURITY EXPLAINED

When it comes to the security of your site, there are two things you need to worry about.

1. The security of your site overall
2. The security of your customers' payment information

The security of your site is important because it controls everything. If someone gained access to your site, they could get all of your customer's email addresses and mailing addresses. They could deface your website and do all sorts of other nefarious things.

The security of your customers' payment information is critical so customers know they can trust you and your company. No one will want to purchase something from you if they think their payment information will be stolen.

So we need to handle both of these.

PROTECTING YOUR LOGIN INFORMATION

The first thing we should do is protect your login information.

I'm writing this at a coffee shop and when I log into my site, I see "https" before my domain name:

The "s" in HTTPS means that the login details are being safely sent from my laptop to the website. If I try to log into my site and it isn't protected by HTTPS, anyone else at this coffee shop could intercept and read my password & username. HTTPS won't keep your website safe from hackers, but it will stop people from stealing your data.

Step 1 to having a secure site is to get an SSL certificate and apply it to your whole site so every page loads in HTTPs. That way when you (or your users) log in, their credentials are protected.

As we mentioned earlier in this book, you can get a free SSL certificate from Let's Encrypt (https://letsencrypt.org). You can contact your host about setting this up for you. They'll usually have fully automated ways for you to do it yourself in a few clicks.

If your host is unwilling to install an SSL certificate for you, find another host.

Step 2 is to protect yourself against brute force attacks. We've already installed Jetpack. They have a fantastic free feature called Protect (https://jetpack.com/support/security-features/). This feature notices if any WordPress sites are being attacked by brute force and will log their IP. It will automatically protect every other WordPress site from those attackers.

It should be turned on automatically once you connect to WordPress.com.

- To make sure it's on, go to your WordPress admin -> "Jetpack" -> "Settings" -> "Security".
- Here you can make sure you're protected against brute force attacks.

PROTECTING YOUR CUSTOMERS' PAYMENT INFORMATION

Now let's look into protecting our users' payment information. Luckily WooCommerce handles most of this for us. With an SSL certificate we protect logins and credit card numbers. Any payment gateway you find on WooCommerce.com will use proper security standards.

You do need to spend a few minutes thinking about PCI compliance. PCI stands for Payment Card Industry. It's the standard for using credit cards in person or online.

You need to fill out a PCI document when you handle credit numbers – even if you aren't personally handling the numbers. With WooCommerce, your payment gateway, such as Stripe, technically handles the credit cards. You can find out more about what exactly WooCommerce handles here: http://ostra.in/woo-pci.

You as a store owner need to fill out a questionnaire stating what you're doing with the numbers. You can find out more about the self assessment questionnaire (SAQ) here: http://ostra.in/woo-assess.

WHAT IS TOKENIZATION?

I do want to talk just a little about saving credit card numbers. If your payment gateway saved physical numbers somewhere, you could be liable for any stolen numbers.

Luckily all good developers know about *tokenization*. They store a token that allows only their store to reuse that credit card number. They don't store the number itself, so it can't be stolen. Any official gateways of WooCommerce.com use tokenization instead of manually storing numbers. I have seen some third party plugins that stored credit card numbers, so before you purchase a third party plugin, be sure to do your research.

When it comes to accepting payment, use some of the free options from WooCommerce.com, such as PayPal or Stripe, or get one of the paid payment gateways. It's better to be safe than sorry when it comes to online payments.

UPDATING YOUR WORDPRESS SITE

It is crucially important is to keep your site up-to-date, including your themes and plugins. When a theme, plugin, or general WordPress update becomes available, try to update it that very day.

I recommend you find a hosting company that really knows and understands WooCommerce. Many hosting companies support dozens of different platforms and know very little about WooCommerce.

WooCommerce-specific hosts don't cost that much more than regular hosts, and they are phenomenal when it comes to security. If you haven't already, check out Nexcess: https://www.nexcess.net/woocommerce/hosting.

WHAT'S NEXT?

With a couple best practices, we've made our store highly secure. It's time to launch your store if you haven't already.

In the next chapter, we'll look at product reviews and how they can help your store. In short: they're awesome and you want as many as possible.

CHAPTER 19.

WOOCOMMERCE REVIEWS EXPLAINED

One of the most important elements on a product page is user generated content. This can take the form of pictures, reviews, star ratings, etc. All of this is called social proof. Social proof is a huge factor in someone else's purchase decision. Getting someone to buy a product from a random website is very hard. If you have a few reviews, that eases people's fears and they'll be more likely to buy.

You want to have reviews for your product. Even negative reviews can be good for your credibility. In a study by Reevoo (http://ostra.in/woo-reviews), 95% of consumers think your reviews are fake if they are all positive. So you shouldn't be too quick to delete or block those negative reviews!

As a new store owner you need to reach out to customers and reviewers to get real reviews of your products. In this chapter, we are going to take a look at product reviews and how you can display them in WooCommerce.

ENABLING REVIEWS

The first step is to make sure reviews are enabled in WooCommerce. They should be on by default, but sometimes plugins can disable this functionality by accident.

- In the admin of your store, click on "WooCommerce" -> "Settings" -> "Products" -> "General".

- If you scroll down, you'll see the "Reviews" settings.

- You can see that product reviews are enabled, so we're good there.

Reviews

Enable reviews	☑ Enable product reviews
	☑ Show "verified owner" label on customer reviews
	☐ Reviews can only be left by "verified owners"
Product ratings	☑ Enable star rating on reviews
	☑ Star ratings should be required, not optional

There are two settings here about 'verified owners' but there isn't a definition. What *is* a verified owner?

A verified owner is someone who purchased the reviewed product from your store. In other words, your store knows they bought that product.

You could discourage reviews by only allowing verified owners to leave reviews, but I don't recommend this. If someone wants to review your product on both Amazon and your store, you want them to be able to do so on both, even though only one store will have that verified owner tag.

WORKING WITH REVIEWERS

If you have a brand new store, it's a good idea to get a few friends, family, and industry experts to review your products. Now I don't recommend sending out products to every possible person. That's an easy way to lose inventory and not get anything from it.

Instead I recommend asking if someone is interested in reviewing. If so, give them a 100% off coupon, plus free shipping for that specific product. That way they can order the product if they're interested, and if they don't order the product, they're clearly not interested enough. And as a bonus they'll be a verified owner on your store.

REVIEWS ON THE FRONT END

Let's make sure reviews work on the front end. They should work fine, but occasionally a theme will not include the right code and reviews aren't possible. Let's check.

- Go to the frontend of your site.

- Navigate to a product.

On most themes, reviews will be tucked away at the bottom of the product page in a tab. But sometimes they may be located somewhere else. If you don't see them on the product page, it's likely your theme doesn't support reviews and I'd reach out to your theme developer.

Let's see what a complete review looks like.

- If your theme displays the reviews in a tab, click the tab.
- Write a review.
- Click "Submit".

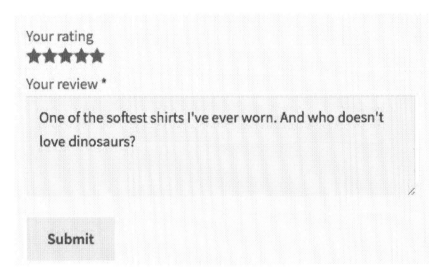

- Now you should see a published review.

The reviews use the WordPress comments system, so all of the things that you already know about comments apply here. I was able to simply give a review without moderation because I'm logged in. If I were not logged in, the review would need to be moderated. Let's take a look at what that look likes.

Your review is awaiting approval   ★★

This shirt was too tight around the neck. Dislike.

Here you can see that when you submit a review, it says that your review is awaiting moderation. Nobody else would be able to see this review until it has been approved.

When you go back to the admin, you'll see that you have one comment awaiting approval.

From here you can choose to "Approve," "Reply," "Edit," "Trash," or mark as "Spam".

If we approve this review, we will be able to see it on our site. You might remember based on WordPress comments, that once an address for a user has been approved, that user is able to post in the future without needing approval.

GOING FURTHER WITH REVIEWS

We've covered the core features of WooCommerce Reviews in this chapter.

There are a few extra things you can do if you really want to have gorgeous reviews. You could look into WooCommerce Product Reviews Pro (http://ostra.in/woo-reviews-pro), which lets users submit additional types of reviews like photos and video reviews as well as submit questions and answers to other users' questions.

If you have an active user base, an extension like this will make your Reviews section quite vibrant.

We also recommend the Customer Reviews for WooCommerce plugin, which is available for free on WordPress.org.

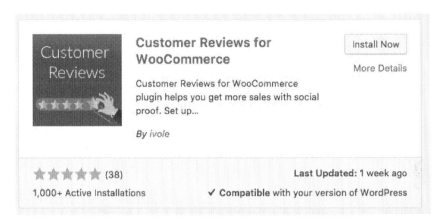

Customer Reviews for WooCommerce has a range of useful features.

- Go to "WooCommerce" -> "Settings" -> "Reviews".

- Here you can set up automatic reminders to ask people for reviews after purchasing a product:

- The email reminder can be customized to maximize your chances of getting a good review:

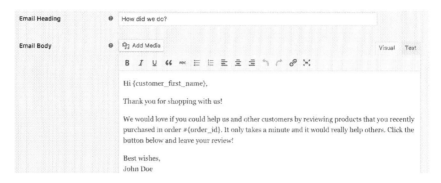

The plugin has a variety of other useful features too. Click the "Review Extensions" tab and you can enable the ability to upload images alongside a review:

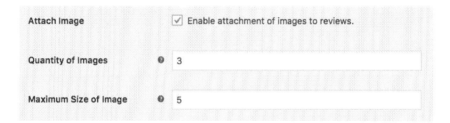

If you want, you can even give customers a discount for leaving a review. Remember the "purplevillelaunch" coupon we created back in the chapter called "WooCommerce Coupons Explained"? Click the "Review for Discount" tab, and you can automatically send this coupon to all your reviewers:

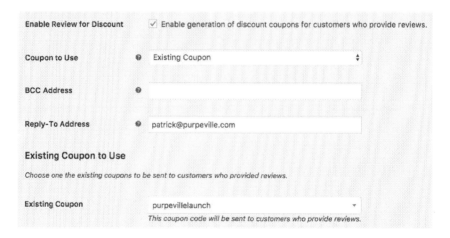

CHAPTER 20.

WHAT'S NEXT?

Congratulations! You've reached the end of the main portion of WooCommerce Explained!

You're now ready to go out and improve your WooCommerce skills.

What should you do next?

- **Practice**. The only way to get better at WooCommerce is to build WooCommerce sites. Decide on your first WooCommerce project and start practicing.

- **Practice now**. You will forget most of what you've read in this book. That's human nature and doesn't make us bad teachers or you a bad learner. The longer you wait to practice WooCommerce, the more you'll forget. Why not start right away?

- **Learn more**. We guarantee that there are things you will come across while using WooCommerce that haven't been included in this book. This book has only a limited number of pages, and we've tried to focus on only the most important things about WooCommerce. We also tried hard to avoid any code so that the barrier to entry for using WooCommerce is as low as possible. However, we do have some bonus chapters for you!

ARE YOU STUCK ON A WOOCOMMERCE PROBLEM?

One of the great things about WooCommerce being so popular is that almost every problem you run into has been encountered by other people. Many of those people will have asked for or posted a solution to their problem online.

If you ever get stuck, here are the first places you should go to for help:

- **Contact us**: Get in touch by emailing books@ostraining.com.

- **Use Google**: If you get an error message or encounter a problem, type it directly into a search engine, and there's a good chance you'll find a solution.

- **Use the WooCommerce help forums**: https://wordpress.org/support/plugin/woocommerce/. The WooCommerce forums have millions of posts, so you can find a lot of solutions. Search for a solution to your question, and if you don't find it, write a new post. There's sure to be someone who can help you.

- **Join the WordPress community**: WordPress doesn't rely on money; it relies on people like you. Whether you attend a local WordPress event, post solutions you find on the forum, or even say thank you to someone who's helped you, there are many easy ways to become part of the WooCommerce community. The more you rely on WooCommerce for your website or your business, the more it can benefit you to become part of the community.
Visit https://central.wordcamp.org for an event near you.

We hope to see you around in the community, and we wish you all the best in your use of WooCommerce!

BONUS CHAPTERS IN THIS BOOK

Yes, the main part of the book has finished, but as an extra treat we've included some bonus chapters.

Why did we not include these chapters in the main part of the book?

- These are topics that are very helpful to know about, but not every WooCommerce user needs to know.
- Rather than following through in a step-by-step order, you can read each of these chapters individually.

The next three chapters cover the WooCommerce settings, some basic programming skills for WooCommerce, and using your store for Point-of-Sale purchases. If any of those topics interest you, turn to the appropriate page and let's learn some more WooCommerce!

CHAPTER 21.

BONUS: WOOCOMMERCE SETTINGS EXPLAINED

In this bonus chapter of this book, we're going to look over the WooCommerce Settings area.

In the main part of the book, we tried to avoid talking about the Settings in-depth. You want to set up your store and get it running. You don't want a detailed tour of all the buttons and options throughout the admin area.

However, we've included a discussion of the Settings as a bonus chapter, because it will be useful to some readers.

Before we begin looking at the settings though, let's check our System Status. The System Status is a tool built into WooCommerce to make sure our system has all the resources that it needs and that nothing is missing. It's kind of like dashboard lights on a car.

STATUS

- In your WordPress admin, go to "WooCommerce" and then "Status".

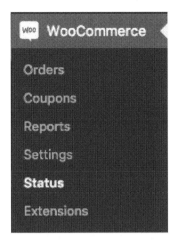

- If there are any errors or mistakes in the setup of your site, WooCommerce reports them here in red text. Luckily for us we see all green.

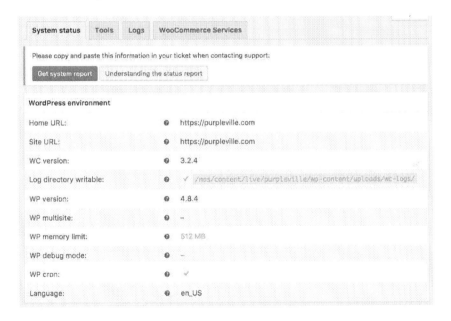

If you do see any red, it's likely going to be the WP memory limit. You can contact your host to help you fix this. Or, WooCommerce has a guide on how to fix that issue: http://ostra.in/woo-memory.

- Click the "Tools" tab up top.

Here you'll find some tools to do things, like "Clear transients," "Install pages," "Delete ALL tax rates," and other useful functions. You probably won't need any of these tools, but they're there in case you accidentally delete an essential WooCommerce page (like the My Account page).

Two other useful tools are the two tools that clear transients. Transients are temporary data in WordPress. If you updated something but you're not seeing the updated version on the front end, you could try clearing your transients.

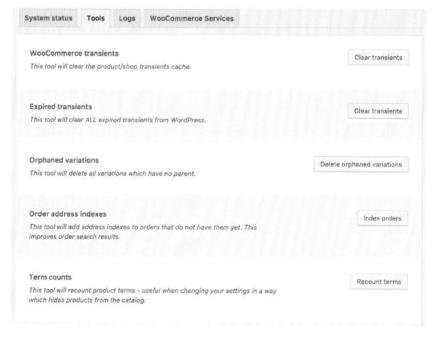

If you are having problems getting live shipping rates or correct taxes through WooCommerce Services, you can test your connection by clicking "Test Connection".

- Click on the "Logs" tab at the top of the page.

- You'll see a screen similar to the one below. Many things are logged here. I can see that my test transaction through Stripe was logged. Again you shouldn't need this information, but just in case something does go wrong, you have many tools to help you solve your own problems.

- Click on the "WooCommerce Services" tab at the top of the page. (You'll only see this if you have both WooCommerce and Jetpack installed.)

- You'll see some data about all of the WooCommerce Services and if they're correctly connected. Everything should be green or yellow (yellow means it's not yet connected or hasn't been used yet).

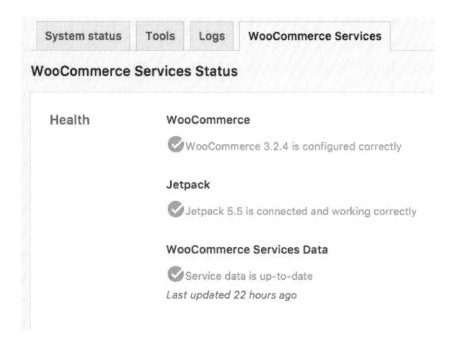

SETTINGS

Now that we know our system status is good to go, let's explore all the options you have with the "Settings" link.

- From the main admin menu, click on "Settings" under "WooCommerce".

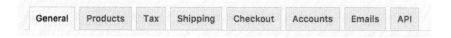

Here you can control the settings for these eight tabs.

- General
- Products
- Tax
- Shipping
- Checkout
- Accounts

- Emails

- API

Let's look at each of them in more detail in the sections below.

SETTINGS: GENERAL TAB

The first tab on the left is for "General" settings. You see that under this tab we can set three main things.

- **Store Address**: Here we can set our "Store Address".

- **General Options:** We can set which countries we want to sell to under "Selling Location(s)". We can set a "Default Customer Address" (useful for shipping estimates). We also have the option to "Enable site-wide store notice text".

- **Currency Options:** Here we can choose whatever "Currency" we wish to use and the "Currency Position". We can also enter a "Thousand Separator," which is a comma in the US, a "Decimal Separator" and the "Number of Decimals". I recommend leaving these as is.

Let's create a site-wide store notice to let our users know we're running a holiday promotion.

- Under "General Options" check "Enable site-wide store notice text".

- Enter a description for our notice.

- Click "Save changes" at the bottom of the page.

Store notice	☑ Enable site-wide store notice text
Store notice text	It's that time of year again for a crazy holiday sale. Enter HOLIDAY at checkout for 10% off.

- Let's see how the store-wide notice appears on our store. As you can see in the image below, at the bottom of our page we see our message. Your theme may choose to display it somewhere else – but either the top or bottom of the page is the most common.

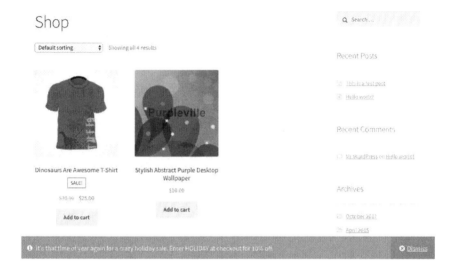

SETTINGS: PRODUCTS TAB

There are four links under the "Products" tab:

- General
- Display
- Inventory
- Downloadable Products

Let's look at each of these.

The "General" Link

- Click "General" and you'll see a screen like the one below.

Measurements

Weight unit	ⓘ	oz ▾
Dimensions unit	ⓘ	in ▾

Reviews

Enable reviews
- ☑ Enable product reviews
- ☑ Show "verified owner" label on customer reviews
- ☐ Reviews can only be left by "verified owners"

Product ratings
- ☑ Enable star rating on reviews
- ☑ Star ratings should be required, not optional

Here we can choose our "Weight unit" and "Dimensions unit". We can also optionally create some settings for our "Reviews".

The "Display" Link

- Click "Display" and you'll see a screen like the one below.

Shop & product pages

Shop page	❷	Shop x ▾
		The base page can also be used in your product permalinks.
Shop page display	❷	Show products ▾
Default category display	❷	Show products ▾
Default product sorting	❷	Default sorting (custom ordering + name) ▾
Add to cart behaviour		☐ Redirect to the cart page after successful addition
		☑ Enable AJAX add to cart buttons on archives

Product images

These settings affect the display and dimensions of images in your catalog – the display on the front-end will still be affected by CSS styles. After changing these settings you may need to regenerate your thumbnails.

Catalog images	❷	300 × 300 px ☑ Hard crop?
Single product image	❷	600 × 600 px ☑ Hard crop?
Product thumbnails	❷	180 × 180 px ☑ Hard crop?

Here we can choose where products are displayed by default. Out of the box, they are displayed on the "Shop" page, but we can change it to any other page that we wish to use.

We could enable the "Redirect to the cart page after successful addition" setting to have our site redirect users to the cart page whenever they add something to their cart. This is a great idea if you only have one product, but otherwise it might annoy people. We also have the option to "Enable AJAX add to cart buttons on archives" so that the entire page doesn't have to reload.

You also see "Default product sorting" on this page. Right now it's set to "custom ordering + name" but we have many other options to choose from.

- Click the arrow to get the dropdown menu, and you'll see a screen like the one below.

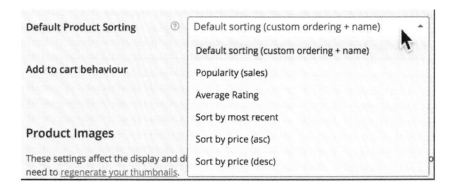

- You see at the bottom of the page we have a section for "Product images".

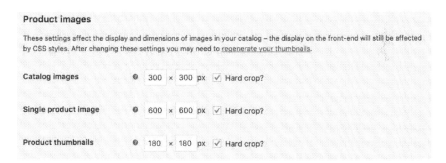

WordPress automatically resizes images when you upload them, but WooCommerce creates some additional sizes, such as "Catalog images," "Single product image," and "Product thumbnails".

The "Inventory" Link

Now let's see what we can do with our "Inventory" link.

- Click "Inventory" and you will see a screen like the one below.

Inventory

Manage stock	☑ Enable stock management
Hold stock (minutes)	60 *Hold stock (for unpaid orders) for x minutes. When this limit is reached, the pending order will be cancelled. Leave blank to disable.*
Notifications	☑ Enable low stock notifications ☑ Enable out of stock notifications
Notification recipient(s)	⊗ ▓▓▓▓@gmail.com
Low stock threshold	⊗ 2
Out of stock threshold	⊗ 0
Out of stock visibility	☐ Hide out of stock items from the catalog
Stock display format	⊗ Always show quantity remaining in stock e.g. "12 in st... ▾

We have the option to completely disable inventory with the "Enable stock managment" choice. We don't have to use it. This might be useful if all your products are digital and we don't actually have inventory, or if we make products on demand.

If you enable inventory and someone puts something in their cart, the "Hold Stock" option will determine how long to keep the product in the customer's cart before releasing it back into inventory. This ensures that another customer isn't able to buy a product out from under your previous customer but also so that if the customer doesn't proceed with the order, the item doesn't continue to sit in their cart.

We can "Enable low stock notifications" and "Enable out of stock notifications". We can also specify the email address for who should be notified.

Here you also have the option to set "Low stock threshold," "Out of stock threshold," and also "Out of stock visibility". You don't have to tell people that you are out of stock, but it is generally a wise thing to do.

You can also specify the "Stock display format" on this page.

The "Downloadable products" Link

We can also control the settings for our "Downloadable products".

- Under the "Products" tab, click "Downloadable products" and you will see a screen like the one below.

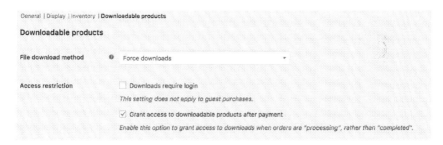

In the past, you may have clicked on a piece of audio and expected the file to download but instead were taken to a page with an audio player, which played the audio. Here we have the option to "Force downloads" rather than let it play in the browser.

If you have any issues downloading files, you can change the "File download method" to "Redirect only". It's less secure but also less problematic.

Under "Access Restriction" we can also set restrictions to the downloadable products once they have been purchased.

SETTINGS: TAX TAB

Taxes can be turned on and off under the "General" tab. Everything else with taxes can be controlled on the Tax tab.

There are four links under the "Tax" tab:

- Tax Options
- Standard Rates
- Reduced Rate Rates
- Zero Rate Rates

Let's look at these in more detail.

- Click "Tax options" and you'll see a screen like the one below.

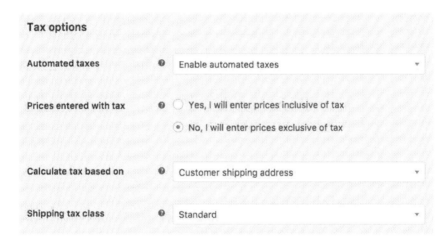

You can choose to enable/disable automated taxes through WooCommerce Services, which I recommend.

You can choose to include or exclude taxes in your prices with the "Yes, I will enter prices inclusive of tax" and "No, I will enter prices exclusive of tax" options. This is entirely up to you, and you are going to have to decide what your customers are going to want.

You can calculate taxes and shipping tax class based on a variety of options from the drop down menus.

Here you can also choose "Round tax at subtotal level, instead of rounding per line".

You also have a variety of options to determine how you will render taxes on the front end.

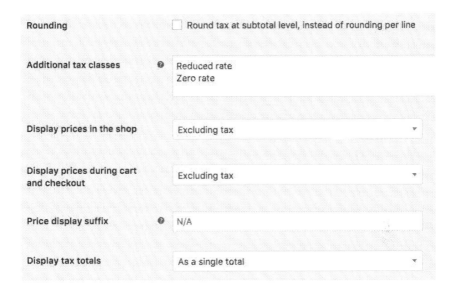

The other links from the top menu allow you to set up "Standard Rates," "Reduced Rate Rates," and "Zero Rate Rates".

If you need to create custom rates, like a special high rate for alcohol or tobacco, you can create your own rates, which we show in the chapter about taxes.

Once again, you are going to need to know your legal requirements for tax before filling this out properly. I can't tell you what those are, but I would recommend that you speak with a tax accountant who deals with e-commerce and find out what is required for you in your area.

SETTINGS: SHIPPING TAB

There are five links under the "Shipping" tab:

- Shipping zones
- Shipping options
- Shipping classes

- Packages
- Shipping labels

Let's check them out.

The "Shipping zones" Link

- Click "Shipping zones" and you'll see a screen like the one below.

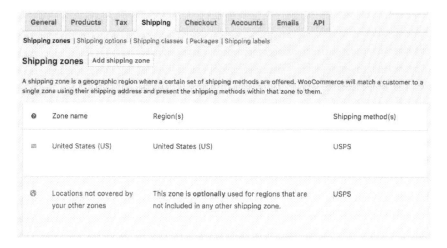

We already covered shipping zones in the welcome wizard. But if you ever want to modify your shipping zones, you can do so here. You can add new zones, modify existing shipping zones, or edit the shipping methods within each zone.

To modify a shipping zone, click into it. Then you can edit the shipping zone or the shipping method. See below for an example.

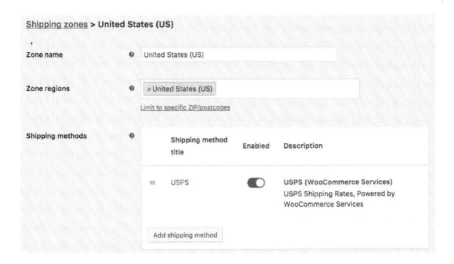

The "Shipping options" Link

- Click on "Shipping options" and you'll see a screen like the one below.

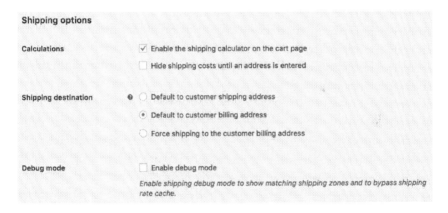

Here we have "Calculations". This lets us display the shipping calculator on the cart page.

"Shipping destination" lets us configure the default address.

"Debug mode" is very useful if you want to see exactly why you're getting specific shipping prices. You can enable this and view the debug message on the cart page.

The "Shipping classes" Link

- Click on "Shipping classes" and you'll see a screen like the one below.

Shipping classes are useful for some advanced shipping customizations. You could have multiple shipping classes for different types of products and use it with an extension like Table Rate Shipping (https://woocommerce.com/products/table-rate-shipping/). But if you use live rate shipping, you shouldn't need to add anything here.

The "Packages" Link

- Click on "Packages" and you should see a screen similar to the one below.

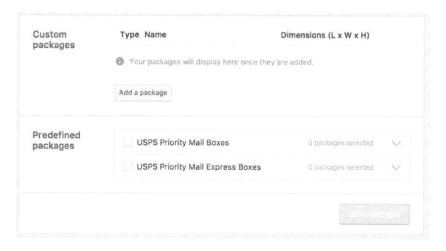

We need to enter all of the packages we'll use to ship our goods. If you have custom packages, you can add them with "Add a package". However, I recommend you use predefined USPS boxes (assuming you're in the United States) since they're generally cheaper.

If you're not in the United States, you may see other predefined boxes here which you can select. If not, you'll have to manually add your own box dimensions.

You can figure out which packages are perfect for you, or it may be easier to enable *all* of the boxes and see what orders come in from your first customers. Then disable the boxes that rarely get used.

• Click the checkbox next to "USPS Priority Mail Boxes" and "USPS Priority Mail Express Boxes". That will enable all of the boxes.

• Click "Save changes".

If you want to select some but not all boxes, click on the down arrow icon to expand them. Then uncheck the boxes you won't use.

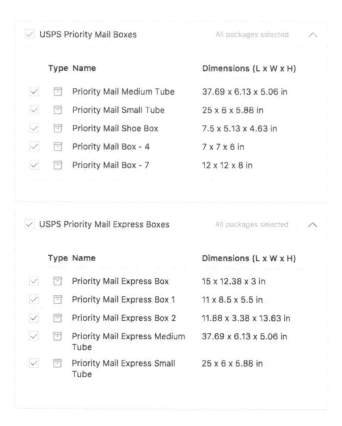

The "Shipping labels" Link

- Click "Shipping labels" and you'll see your billing information that's saved on WordPress.com.

- We can select our label size under "Paper size". You'll want to keep it set to "Letter" until you purchase a special label printer that has smaller paper.

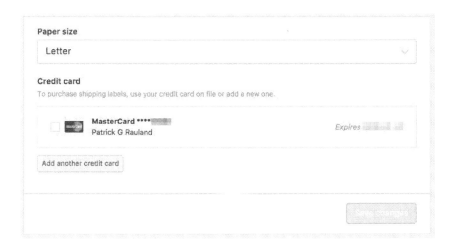

SETTINGS: CHECKOUT TAB

There are six links under the "Checkout" tab:

- Checkout Options
- BACS
- Check payments
- Cash on delivery
- PayPal
- Stripe

Let's look at these in more detail.

- Click "Checkout Options" and you'll see a screen like the one below.

Checkout process

Coupons	☑ Enable the use of coupons
	Coupons can be applied from the cart and checkout pages.
	☐ Calculate coupon discounts sequentially
	When applying multiple coupons, apply the first coupon to the full price and the second coupon to the discounted price and so on.
Checkout process	☑ Enable guest checkout
	Allows customers to checkout without creating an account.
	☑ Force secure checkout
	Force SSL (HTTPS) on the checkout pages (an SSL Certificate is required).
	☐ Force HTTP when leaving the checkout

You see that here we can set four things:

- **Checkout process:** Here we can "Enable the use of coupons" and enable whether we want to "Calculate coupon discounts sequentially". If you disable "Enable guest checkout," customers must be signed in to checkout. You also have the option to "Force secure checkout". I *highly* recommend this because you want to ensure that the checkout is going to be secure.

- **Checkout Pages:** You can set the "Cart Page," Checkout Page," and "Terms and Conditions". The cart and checkout should be done for you, and you can leave them set to the default. You may want to add a Terms and Conditions page. You can create a regular WordPress page and then come back to this page and select it from the dropdown.

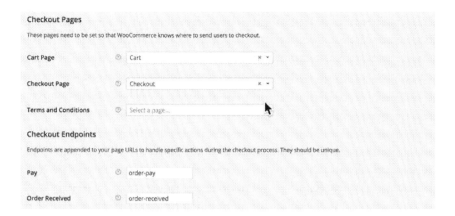

- **Checkout Endpoints:** You can also set the "Checkout Endpoints," which are things that get added to the end of the URL to tell WooCommerce what's supposed to happen on that page. I recommend leaving them alone, unless you really know what you are doing and you want to use something other than the default.

- **Payment gateways:** Here we can choose the order in which payment gateways are listed.

- I'd like to move "Credit Card" to the top so it's the default. Click and drag "Credit Card" to the top of the list.

- Then click "Save changes".

Payment gateways

Installed gateways are listed below. Drag and drop gateways to control their display order on the frontend.

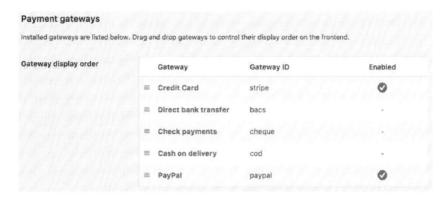

Gateway display order

Gateway	Gateway ID	Enabled
Credit Card	stripe	✓
Direct bank transfer	bacs	-
Check payments	cheque	-
Cash on delivery	cod	-
PayPal	paypal	✓

- In the remaining links under the "Checkout" tab, we can choose settings for each individual payment gateway.

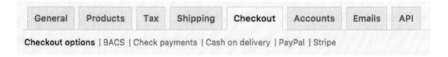

| General | Products | Tax | Shipping | Checkout | Accounts | Emails | API |

Checkout options | BACS | Check payments | Cash on delivery | PayPal | Stripe

If you use a different payment gateway through another plugin or something similar, you should see their payment settings in the menu above.

SETTINGS: ACCOUNTS TAB

- Click the "Accounts" tab, and you'll see a screen like the one below.

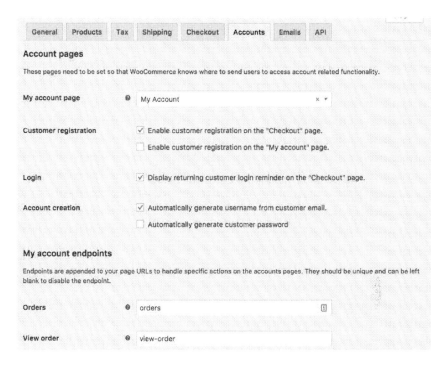

The "Accounts" page refers to end user accounts, such as people who are logged into your site. The "My Account Page" is currently set to "My Account," but again you could create a new page and call it anything you like and set it here in the account settings.

You can also set "My account endpoints". These are similar to the others in that they get added to the URL to tell WooCommerce what's supposed to happen on that particular page.

My account endpoints

Endpoints are appended to your page URLs to handle specific actions on the accounts pages. They should be unique and can be left blank to disable the endpoint.

Orders	❷	orders
View order	❷	view-order
Downloads	❷	downloads
Edit account	❷	edit-account
Addresses	❷	edit-address
Payment methods	❷	payment-methods
Lost password	❷	lost-password
Logout	❷	customer-logout

Here you can also modify the "Registration Options".

- You can "Enable customer registration on the 'Checkout' page" or "Enable customer registration on the 'My account' page".

- You can optionally "Display returning customer login reminder on the 'Checkout' page".

- When an account is created, we can "Automatically generate username from the customer's email address". We can also choose to "Automatically generate customer password".

We don't want to automatically generate usernames from customer's emails, so let's turn that off.

- Uncheck "Automatically generate username from customer email".

- Click "Save changes".

Customer registration	☑ Enable customer registration on the "Checkout" page.
	☐ Enable customer registration on the "My account" page.
Login	☑ Display returning customer login reminder on the "Checkout" page.
Account creation	☐ Automatically generate username from customer email.
	☐ Automatically generate customer password

SETTINGS: EMAILS TAB

WooCommerce sends a variety emails. For example, WooCommerce automatically sends an email to a customer when they've made a new order or when they want to reset their password.

All of these emails except one are on by default. You can see what the email is called, what type of email it is, and the recipient.

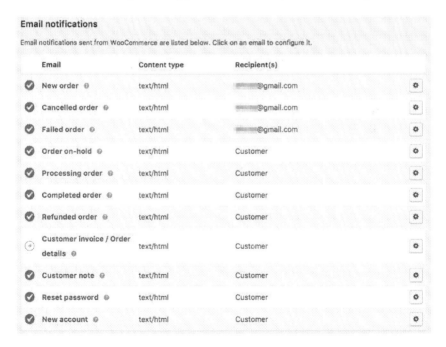

Email notifications

Email notifications sent from WooCommerce are listed below. Click on an email to configure it.

	Email	Content type	Recipient(s)	
✅	New order ⊚	text/html	▓▓▓@gmail.com	⚙
✅	Cancelled order ⊚	text/html	▓▓▓@gmail.com	⚙
✅	Failed order ⊚	text/html	▓▓▓@gmail.com	⚙
✅	Order on-hold ⊚	text/html	Customer	⚙
✅	Processing order ⊚	text/html	Customer	⚙
✅	Completed order ⊚	text/html	Customer	⚙
✅	Refunded order ⊚	text/html	Customer	⚙
⊕	Customer invoice / Order details ⊚	text/html	Customer	⚙
✅	Customer note ⊚	text/html	Customer	⚙
✅	Reset password ⊚	text/html	Customer	⚙
✅	New account ⊚	text/html	Customer	⚙

We could click into any of these emails and change the content of the email.

- Click "Processing order" so we can edit that email.

You'll see you can do the following here:

- Easily edit the details of this email.
- Enable/disable the email entirely.
- Customize the subject.
- Customize the heading within the email.
- Control the email type.

I recommend leaving all of the default emails on. They're all very useful and customers expect them.

We can put a bit of personality into our "Subject" and "Email heading":

- Change "Subject" to "Your Products From {site_title} Will Be With You Soon".
- Change "Email heading" to "We're glad you love purple as much as we do".
- Keep the "Email type" as is. We could change it to a text only email. But generally we want to include our brand colors in our email, which we'll customize in a minute.

- Click "Save changes".

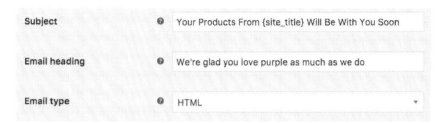

Notice that at the bottom of this page we can customize this email even more by customizing a template. If you're familiar with HTML and PHP, you can customize your email templates this way. If you're not, I recommend hiring a developer to do this for you. Or you might want to look into the WooCommerce Email Customizer (https://woocommerce.com/products/woocommerce-email-customizer/).

- Click the blue arrow by the email name to go to the previous page.
- Scroll down to see more email settings.

Email sender options

"From" name	❷	Purpleville
"From" address	❷	▓▓▓▓@gmail.com

Email template

This section lets you customize the WooCommerce emails. Click here to preview your email template.

Header image	❷	N/A
Footer text	❷	Purpleville
Base color	❷	#96588a
Background color	❷	#f7f7f7
Body background color	❷	#ffffff
Body text color	❷	#3c3c3c

We can also customize the following:

- "From" name
- "From" address in our emails
- Header image
- Footer text

Since these are going to be the default settings for your emails, I recommend making them as clear as possible.

You can also change the colors for the email, including the following:

- Base color
- Background color
- Body background color
- Body text color

Make sure these colors match your brand colors. Since our Purpleville store uses a darker purple, I'll change that.

- Click on the color next to "Base color" and either type in the hexcode or use the color selector.

Now let's preview our email.

- Click "Click here to preview your email template".

HTML email template

Lorem ipsum dolor sit amet, consectetur adipiscing elit. Sed aliquet diam a facilisis eleifend. Cras ac justo felis. Mauris faucibus, orci eu blandit fermentum, lorem nibh sollicitudin mi, sit amet interdum metus urna ut lacus.

Phasellus quis varius augue. Fusce eu euismod leo, a accumsan tellus. Quisque vitae dolor eu justo cursus egestas. Cum sociis natoque penatibus et magnis dis parturient montes, nascetur ridiculus mus. Sed sit amet sapien odio. Sed pellentesque arcu mi, quis malesuada lectus lacinia et. Cras a tempor leo.

Lorem ipsum dolor

Fusce eu euismod leo, a accumsan tellus. Quisque vitae dolor eu justo cursus egestas. Cum sociis natoque penatibus et magnis dis parturient montes, nascetur ridiculus mus. Sed sit amet sapien odio. Sed pellentesque arcu mi, quis malesuada lectus lacinia et. Cras a tempor leo.

Purpleville

Looks pretty good for just pressing a couple buttons.

- Click "Save changes" when you're done.

SETTINGS: API TAB

There are three links under the "API" tab:

- Settings
- Keys/Apps
- Webhooks

Let's look at these in more detail.

- Click "Settings" and you'll see a screen like the one below.

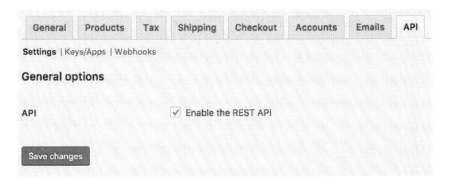

This lets us "Enable the REST API". An API allows someone to create an application that uses the data from your store. You could create your own mobile application for your store, and it would use WordPress as the backend.

Some extensions or third party services will require that you enable the REST API and create an API key on the "Keys/Apps" tab. Some applications may have you create a webhook under the "Webhooks" tab.

Either way, follow their instructions to either create the API key or webhook.

CHAPTER 22.

BONUS: WOOCOMMERCE PROGRAMMING EXPLAINED

Welcome to the second bonus chapter of this book.

Throughout this book, we've avoided using any code. We believe that anyone is able to build a great WooCommerce site.

In this chapter, we are going to talk about some WooCommerce programming basics. If you're not interested in coding, please feel free to skip this chapter.

YOUR FIRST WOOCOMMERCE CODE CHANGE

Let's tackle our first WooCommerce code change. I'd like to add some text to the "Cart" page, right underneath the mean heading.

There is no way to do this using the WooCommerce admin area, so I'm going to look at the plugin files. We're going to look for a logically named file called cart.php inside our WooCommerce templates folder.

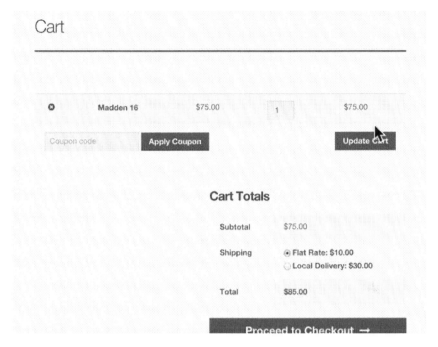

Cart

| | Madden 16 | $75.00 | 1 | $75.00 |

Coupon code   **Apply Coupon**   **Update Cart**

Cart Totals

Subtotal	$75.00
Shipping	⊙ Flat Rate: $10.00
	○ Local Delivery: $30.00
Total	$85.00

Proceed to Checkout →

- Log into your WordPress site files.

- Go to /wp-content/, then /plugins/.

- Open the /woocommerce/ folder, then open /templates/ and finally /cart/.

- Select the file called cart.php and open it in your text editor.

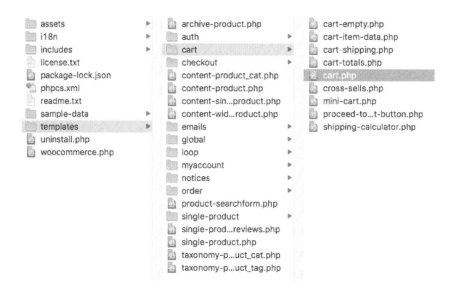

- This next image shows the first 40 lines of the cart.php file:

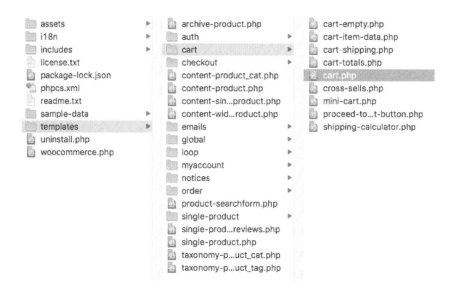

- There is a lazy way to add our text to the Cart page. We could simply write "Hi there" directly into the file, as on Line 17 below:

```
cart.php                    x
 1  <?php
 2  /**
 3   * Cart Page
 4   *
 5   * @author  WooThemes
 6   * @package WooCommerce/Templates
 7   * @version 2.3.8
 8   */
 9
10  if ( ! defined( 'ABSPATH' ) ) {
11      exit; // Exit if accessed directly
12  }
13
14  wc_print_notices();
15
16  do_action( 'woocommerce_before_cart' ); ?>
17  Hi there
18
19  <form action="<?php echo esc_url( WC()->cart->get_cart_url() ); ?>" method="post">
20
21  <?php do_action( 'woocommerce_before_cart_table' ); ?>
22
```

- This lazy change really does work. If you save the cart.php file with this new text, you can refresh your "Cart" screen and it does show on your site.

Cart

Hi there

| ● | Madden 16 | $75.00 | 1 | $75.00 |

| Coupon code | Apply Coupon | | | Update Cart |

Cart Totals

Subtotal	$75.00
Shipping	● Flat Rate: $10.00
	○ Local Delivery: $30.00

However, this lazy approach has some significant drawbacks. If you update WooCommerce, it will remove your code change. You could avoid this by copying the cart.php file to your main theme folder.

Nonetheless, my favorite (and the most elegant) approach is to use a hook. This right here, woocommerce_before_cart, is a hook. This allows me to run some code in that spot.

```
14   wc_print_notices();
15
16   do_action( 'woocommerce_before_cart' ); ?>
17   |
```

In this chapter, I'm going to recommend that we create a plugin to put our text here.

Yes, you could write this code in your theme's function.php file. However, if your theme ever gets updated or changed, then your code is gone. Another advantage of using a plugin is that it's very easy to activate or deactivate from the "Plugins" screen inside WordPress.

This is not a book about writing WordPress plugins, so we're going to use a helpful plugin: https://wordpress.org/plugins/pluginception. Pluginception allows you to easily create a new blank plugin in WordPress.

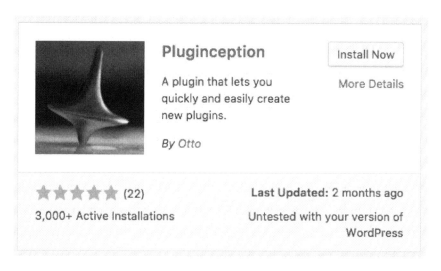

Keep in mind that adding code for WordPress can easily cause a white screen of death, particularly as you're testing your code.

You really don't want to do this on your live site. So, please use the testing site you've been working on throughout this book.

- Go to "Plugins" in your site. Search for and install "Plugineception".

- Under the "Plugins" link, you'll see a "Create a New Plugin" link.

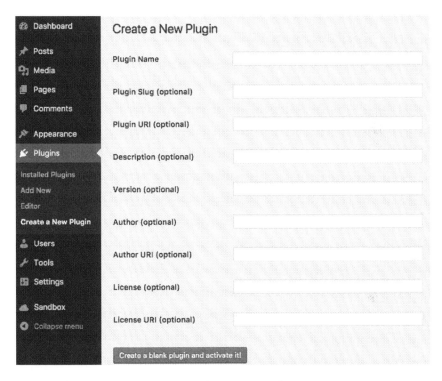

We really have two options here. Our first option is to create one plugin for all of our code snippets. We could call it our WooCommerce plugin. The disadvantage is that if you ever need to deactivate part of the code, you have to edit the plugin. If we make a different plugin for each change we want to do, then it's easy to turn them on or off individually. Sometimes people have a fear of having too many plugins and slowing down WordPress with it. In reality, the number of plugins has nothing to do with WordPress' speed. They key to a fast site is the quality of code in your plugin. If you have one terribly-written plugin, it will slow everything down, but if you have 10,000 excellent plugins your site should not be slow at all.

- On the "Create a New Plugin" screen, the only required field is the "Plugin Name". All of the other fields are optional.

- Click "Create a new plugin and activate it!" when you're finished.

Create a New Plugin

Plugin Name	Patrick's Text Above the WooCommerce Cart
Plugin Slug (optional)	
Plugin URI (optional)	
Description (optional)	
Version (optional)	1.0
Author (optional)	Patrick

- WordPress will now show you a warning. Read this carefully. What we're about to do is definitely not wise on a live site, but we'll be fine on our test site.

- Click "I understand".

Heads up!

You appear to be making direct edits to your plugin in the WordPress dashboard. We recommend that you don't! Editing plugins directly may introduce incompatibilities that break your site and your changes may be lost in future updates.

If you absolutely have to make direct edits to this plugin, use a file manager to create a copy with a new name and hang on to the original. That way, you can re-enable a functional version if something goes wrong.

`Go back`   `I understand`

- To prove that it is there, I will go to plugins, and sure enough you can see our newly created plugin.

Edit Plugins

Editing patricks-text-above-the-woocommerce-cart/patricks-t

Selected file content:

```
 1  <?php
 2  /*
 3  Plugin Name: Patrick's Text Above the WooCommerce Cart
 4  Plugin URI:
 5  Description:
 6  Version: 1.0
 7  Author: Patrick
 8  Author URI:
 9  License:
10  License URI:
11  */
12
```

- Inside the plugin editor, I'm going to write the code for our plugin:

```
 7 Author: Patrick
 8 Author URI:
 9 License:
10 License URI:
11 */
12
13 function patrick_woocart_prefix() {
14     echo "You have been eaten by a Grue.";
15 }
16 add_action( 'woocommerce_before_cart', 'patrick_woocart_prefix' );
```

First, we define a function. We need to give the function a unique name that no-one else will ever use, so I'm using my personal name: patrick_woocart_prefix. This function simply echoes "You have been eaten by a Grue" which is a joke taken from Zork, an old computer game: https://en.wikipedia.org/wiki/Zork.

Second, I will call the function add_action. I am taking the woocommerce_before_cart action that we saw earlier on Line 16 from our cart.php file. Next, I'm including the function we just defined.

- Click "Update file".

- Visit the front of your site, and you'll see the new text on your Cart screen:

Cart

You have been eaten by a Grue.

⚙	Madden 16	$75.00	1	$75.00

Coupon code	**Apply Coupon**		**Update Cart**

Cart Totals

Subtotal	$75.00
Shipping	⦿ Flat Rate: $10.00
	◯ Local Delivery: $30.00

You can now use this plugin to write anything you want. It could be an announcement, a special offer, or anything else that you wish. To remove this text, you can simply disable the plugin.

This approach is a personal preference, and I know some other WordPress developers disagree. However, I really prefer to create small plugins with specific tasks rather than one giant plugin that has multiple purposes.

DESIGNING YOUR WOOCOMMERCE SITE

In this part of the chapter, we're going to look at how to style WooCommerce.

Here is our cart, and you can see that we have a big purple "Process to Checkout" button. Let's show you how to change the color of that button.

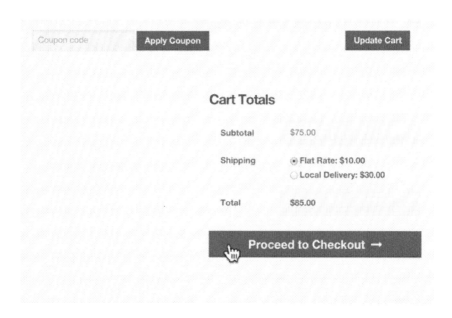

There is a new plugin called WooCommerce Colors that allows you to change the buttons color and other elements of WooCommerce. This plugin integrates with the WordPress customizer. Let's install this plugin and see how it looks.

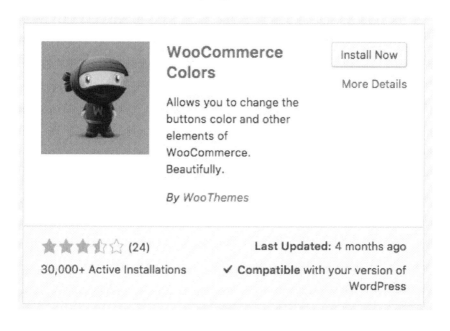

- Once we have the WooCommerce Colors plugin installed, go to "Appearance" then "Customize".
- There will now be two "WooCommerce" links in the Customizer menu. Click on the top "WooCommerce" link:

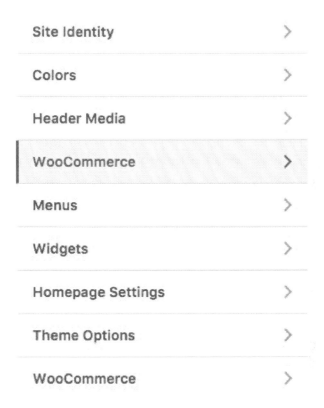

- Here you can change the "Primary Color" of your WooCommerce store. By default, it is set to a purple color: #a46497.

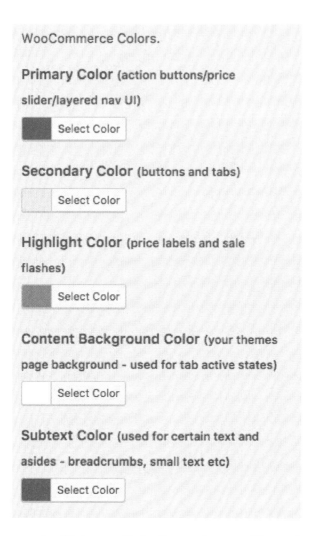

WooCommerce Colors.

Primary Color (action buttons/price slider/layered nav UI)

Select Color

Secondary Color (buttons and tabs)

Select Color

Highlight Color (price labels and sale flashes)

Select Color

Content Background Color (your themes page background - used for tab active states)

Select Color

Subtext Color (used for certain text and asides - breadcrumbs, small text etc)

Select Color

If you change the "Primary Color" to red, you will see that change automatically reflected on the screen. Notice also that the "Secondary Color" automatically changes so that we can still read the text in the button.

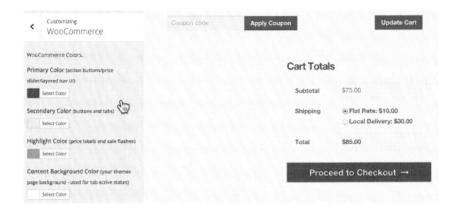

The "WooCommerce Colors" plugin is one of the simplest ways to change some of the elements of WooCommerce.

Also in the WordPress Customizer, you find an "Additional CSS" area. You can use this area to add your own CSS.

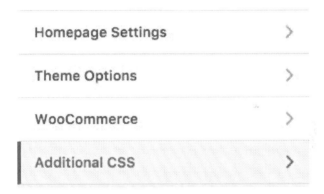

The other option is to edit the style.css file in your theme. I would highly recommend using a child theme so it won't get overwritten when your theme updates. This tutorial has recommendations on creating a child theme: http://ostra.in/woo-child.

CHANGING EMAIL TEMPLATES

In this final part of the chapter, we are going to look at editing email templates.

Before we edit the templates, let's get a feel for what they look like.

- Go to "WooCommerce" then "Orders".

- Either find an order for your account, or create new order. We want an order that is associated with our email address.

- Using the "Order actions" option in the top-right, choose "Resend new order notification":

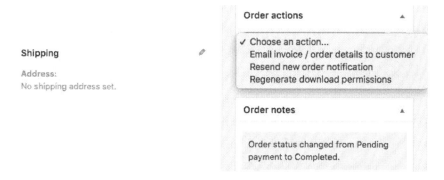

- Check your inbox, and you'll see what the order email looks like:

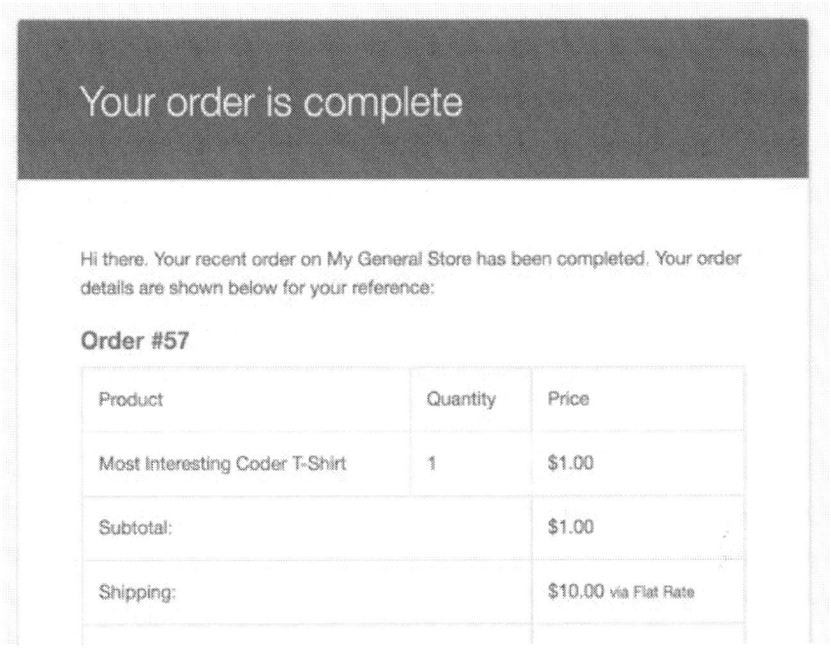

Your order is complete

Hi there. Your recent order on My General Store has been completed. Your order details are shown below for your reference:

Order #57

Product	Quantity	Price
Most Interesting Coder T-Shirt	1	$1.00
Subtotal:		$1.00
Shipping:		$10.00 via Flat Rate

There are a limited amount of things that you can do to this template within the WooCommerce admin interface.

- Go to "WooCommerce" -> "Settings" -> "Emails".
- Scroll down a little. Here you can customize some global settings for all your emails, including the 'From' name and address, a Header image, and the Footer text.

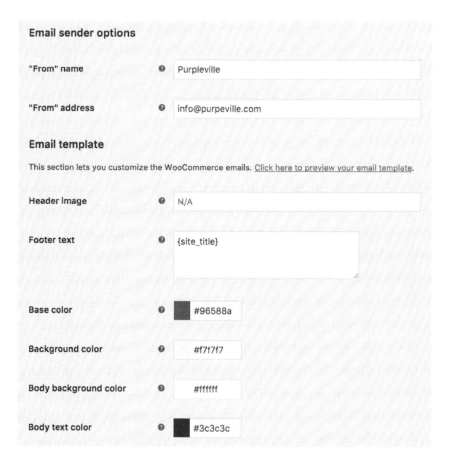

At the top of the "Emails screen," you can see links for a wide variety of email templates.

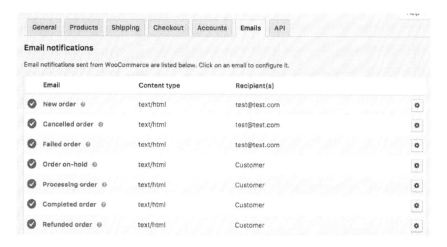

- Click on the cog icon on the right-hand side next to "New order".

Here you can edit the Recipients, Subject, Email heading and Email type. WooCommerce will also tell you the exact file you can use to edit this email.

- Click "Copy file to theme". This will automatically create a copy of the file for you inside your theme's folder.

- Open up the file system for your WooCommerce site.

- Browse to your new WooCommerce files, whose location you saw in the previous step. In the image above, the location would be wp-content/themes/twentyseventeen/woocommerce/emails/

- Open the copy of the admin-new-order.php file.

At the top of the file there is a woocommerce_email_header hook. Earlier in this chapter we used a very similar action hook. In this instance, WooCommerce itself uses this action to put the email header image into this template:

```php
<?php        do_action(         'woocommerce_email_header',
$email_heading ); ?>
```

The text I want to change is shown in the image below. This text is hardcoded in Line 18 of the admin-new-order.php file. Because this file has been copied and stored in our theme folder, we can edit this text directly. If you change the text, you can see how it looks by returning to the WordPress admin area and resending yourself the email.

Hi there Chris. Your recent order on My General Store has been completed. Your order details are shown below for your reference:

Using this method you could edit anything in this template. You could add a row to the HTML table, you could further customize the greeting, you could take advantage of hooks or anything else you may need.

This process can be repeated for any WooCommerce email template. Go to the WooCommerce settings, pick the email that you want to edit and then copy the template to your theme. You don't necessarily have to know PHP. You could change some of the words in the file using plain English.

CHAPTER 23.

BONUS: WOOCOMMERCE POINT-OF-SALE EXPLAINED

WooCommerce is the most popular way to build an online store. Square is the most popular way to build a point-of-sale solution in many countries. Why not bring the two together?

That's the idea behind the new Square for WooCommerce plugin. This was the most popular requested feature by WooCommerce customers.

Here's an overview of how the Square integration works with WooCommerce.

To get started, you'll need your WooCommerce site, plus a Square account and one of their card readers. This image below shows some of the Point-of-Sale readers that Square offers:

Stand   Contactless + chip reader   Magstripe reader

- Download the free WooCommerce Square integration.

- Install the integration by going to your WordPress site-> "Plugins" -> "Upload Plugin".

- After installation, you'll see a black "Connect with Square" plugin.

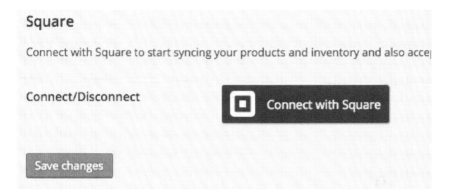

- You'll now be taken to Square.com and will be asked to grant permissions.

- Click "Allow".

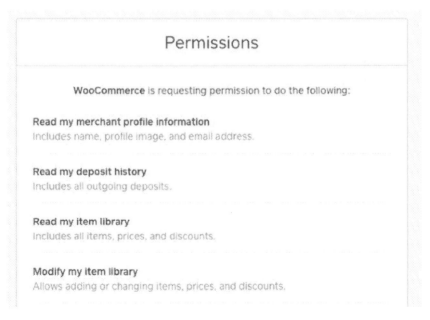

- Click to be redirected back to your WordPress site.

- Go to "WooCommerce" -> "Settings" -> "Integration".
- You'll see the Square sync settings. You can choose to sync Categories, Inventory, Images and more.

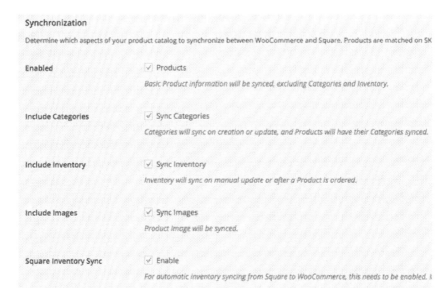

At the bottom of the screen, you can also do a manual sync:

It's worth taking time to understand how these sync settings work:

- Auto-sync is only available for inventory. You will need to manually sync changes for categories, images and other items.

- Square only allows one category per product, so WooCommerce will be forced to chose one per product also.

Also, pay attention to the direction of the sync:

- Any changes you make to your inventory in WooCommerce will be immediately synced to Square.

- Any changes you make to your inventory in Square will be synced hourly to WooCommerce.

So there is a difference here. WooCommerce to Square is automatic, but the other direction is hourly. It's worth reading through the WooCommerce documentation.

Using Square for online payments

You also decide to use Square for online payments so you don't have to use different gateways for online and offline payments.

- Go to "WooCommerce" -> "Settings" -> "Checkout" -> "Square".

- You can enable Square payments on your site.

- If you check "Create Customer," your online customer will also be synced to Square.

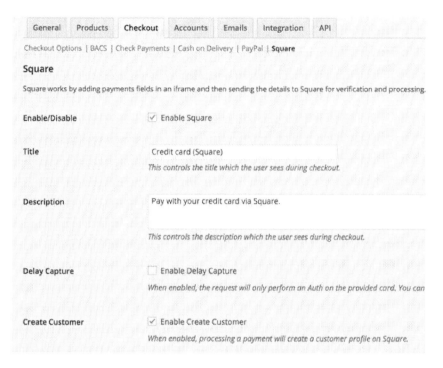

Here's how a credit card checkout form will appear on your site:

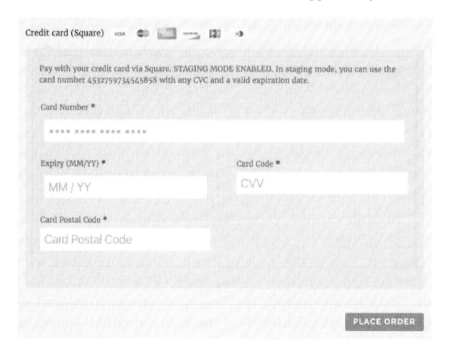

Summary

This is a good start and should encourage many retail sellers to consider WooCommerce. There are some limitations to consider.

- Not all data is synced between WooCommerce and Square.
- The extension is only supported in the US and Canada.
- This a good but a somewhat limited first version. Expect a lot of extra features soon, particularly if it proves a popular product for WooCommerce.

Overall, WooCommerce Square is a very useful product and works well.

At the end of the day, you'll probably need to choose whether Square or WooCommerce is your primary tool. Both of these systems have a lot of overlap in terms of reporting, customer data, email marketing and so on. You will need to choose whether to use Square or WordPress features for those tasks. I suspect that if the majority of your business is online, you'll rely on WordPress. If the majority of your business is offline, you'll stick with Square.

But if your business is both online and offline, Square for WooCommerce is a great place to start.

Printed in Great Britain
by Amazon